The JOY Experiments

Reimagining Mid-sized Cities to Heal Our Divided Society

Scott Higgins & Paul Kalbfleisch

Foreword by Mouna Andraos and Melissa Mongiat, Daily tous les jours

DUNDURN PRESS

BECAUSE CITIES

ARE

IMPORTANT

CHANGING CITIES

CHANGES
THE WORLD

A Note from the Authors

Many of the ideas discussed in this book predate the Covid-19 pandemic. At that time, our focus was on how to create vitality and identity within mid-sized cities such as the Regional Municipality of Waterloo where we live. We had a sense that society was at odds with itself, and everyone was in ideological bunkers and very suspicious of strangers. In some small way, we also believed fresh city building and public-space tactics could make a positive difference. But then the pandemic descended upon the world, seemingly accelerating all the issues society was grappling with … and not always in a good way. Social alarm bells began to go off as society started to realize how divided it was and we all chanted, "We're all in this together," though few had any idea what "together" meant or how to get there as people emptied store shelves of toilet paper.

The majority of *The Joy Experiments* was written during the Covid-19 period, and as a result the book's perspective changed. We saw that cities weren't just about employment and quality of life for the individual; they were becoming a critical mechanism for helping the world move forward in a post-pandemic era. We concluded that the best place for the idea of "together" to get a meaningful foothold in society was in cities and communities rather than at the national or international level. Cities of all sizes have historically contained the infrastructure for nurturing the human spirit, and if we want a world where the best aspects of the human spirit are valued, we need to think about building cities differently than in recent years.

That change in perspective was a journey for us. We hope this book is also a rewarding journey for you. The Contents is set up somewhat like a map. We invite you to take whatever path through the book you feel you need, though we do suggest you follow us closely for the first few chapters. Our hope is that *The Joy Experiments* helps create a common discussion — with common goals for politicians, citizens, architects, city planners, and business leaders — on what we want and need from our cities. This common ground may at first feel strange to everyone. There's no attempt to be academic or to define joy in terms of sunshine and unicorns. Common words are important, because if we can find them, we can also discover the way to better cities.

CONTENTS

1 **Foreword** by Mouna Andraos and Melissa Mongiat, Daily tous les jours

3 **Before You Begin**

4 **Introduction:** Because Cities Are Important

8 ONE **Under Attack: The Decline of the City Habitat**
Cities are the habitat for the human spirit and are every bit as interconnected as nature's habitats. We know natural habitats need protection, so why aren't we also safeguarding human habitats?

22 TWO **The Redesign of "We"**
In the backs of our minds as we worked on our projects, we debated what we liked about cities and what we wanted to change. This thought, or concern, grew over time, evolving and influencing our philosophy and the purpose of our work.

32 THREE **Starting the Journey**
Here we outline the issues and big themes in this book. It's not exactly an executive summary, but it's a great place to start looking differently at the world and the cities around us.

42 FOUR **Bring Your Own City**
The city-building playbook changes when people don't always have to choose where they live based on who they work for. The cities that offer joy have a leg up on the competition in a new game.

56 FIVE **Cities that Offer Joy Win**
LIVE, WORK, PLAY is the current city-building formula. What's the formula for joy? Here's a hint — shuffle the deck.

68 SIX **The Elevator Pitch of a City**
Stories are far more important than we think. In fact, culture is nothing more than the stories we choose to tell about ourselves and the stories we use to determine who we, as communities, will become.

84 SEVEN **You Attract What You Celebrate: Learning How to Claim Our Identity**
The chapter title tells half the story. The other half is that what you don't celebrate you forget and slowly lose. Being humble is a nice virtue … in moderation.

100 EIGHT **The Yardstick Is Youth**
Drive through the country and you'll eventually see towns where young people have come to believe their future exists somewhere else. Investing in the next generation is investing in a city's future.

112 NINE **Experimental Journeys: Eliminating Old Ideas that Obstruct New Ones**
We rarely get to somewhere new by doing the same things over and over. But isn't experimenting risky and don't creative ideas belong to … creative people? Actually, both experimentation and creativity are processes rather than whim-and-eureka moments. A lot of experimentation has to do with finding out what doesn't work. We have a lot that isn't working right now, so that part of building a better world should be easy.

122 TEN **There Is Nothing Wrong with a Big Idea**
Sometimes we just have to go big. *Meander*, a living architecture sculpture, was our big idea, and we learned a lot. It started guiding much of our thinking. That's the beauty and power of big ideas.

136 ELEVEN **Fifty Bright Ideas Are Better Than One**
How do you define collaboration and what happens when it changes from being a tactic for city building to becoming the goal?

150 TWELVE **The Streets Should Be Free**
Historically, the most vibrant areas of cities, the ones where all the new ideas come from, have also been the cheapest areas in which to live — old factories turned into artist lofts, et cetera. So with bricks-and-mortar retail stores in decline and no longer a dependable ingredient for building vibrant streets, why not create free space for human inventiveness? Say what?

162 THIRTEEN **Becoming a Congregation**
Our parents told us not to play with strangers, but in an age in which people are increasingly isolated due to the negative effects of technology, and depression is very common, maybe playing in public isn't such a bad idea.

176 FOURTEEN **The 15-Minute City: How Can We Get There from Here?**
Living in a community where everything you need is only a walk away seems like something everyone would want. So why don't we have it? Sometimes looking for a big solution to a big problem prevents us from reaching our goals step by step.

188 FIFTEEN **Community Is the New Faith**
Many people are placing their hopes and faith in the idea of community, a place where they can feel connected and somewhat in control. And that's a really good thing. But let's also turn our faith into action.

198 **In Closing: Joy Is Practical**

203 **Acknowledgements**

205 **Appendix: The Joy Shift: A New Model for Thinking About, Designing, and Building Cities Differently**

211 **About the Authors and Illustrator**

Foreword

For the past 15 years, Daily tous les jours has been creating large-scale interventions in the public realm to bring people of all ages and backgrounds together in a spirit of collaboration in places as diverse as Detroit and Singapore, Budapest and North Carolina. Our practice combines interactive art, storytelling, performance, and urban design. Everywhere we go, we're humbled by the warm welcome we're greeted with and the commitment of our hosts to overcome all the technical and financial hurdles they encounter to enable us to do our work.

It probably takes a bit of folly to commission Daily tous les jours, as well as a desire to push the boundaries and believe that things can be done differently. Through the hundreds of conversations we have every year with planners, civil servants, community organizers, and city builders, few have as clear and determined a vision as Scott Higgins and Paul Kalbfleisch.

We first found a message from Scott in our inbox in early 2018. Five years later, Scott's vision, paired with Paul's craftsmanship, has brought to life some of our most ambitious work to date. But we're most grateful for the conversations and exchanges we've had the chance to engage in over those years. Although very different, our professional lives have led us to a similar conclusion that our contribution to making the world a better place has to be through bringing more joy into people's daily experiences of their cities.

Sometime in the summer of 2020, amid a global pandemic crisis, when bringing people close to one another in public spaces became illegal and our beloved city of Montreal was ranked the seventh deadliest place in the world, we had a phone call with Paul.

It was ironic then that our survival hinged on our ability to co-operate with strangers, all the while finding ourselves isolated and distrusting one another more than ever before. Paul and Daily tous les jours spoke about the importance of congregations and how we missed them. A city without humans wasn't a city. We needed joy. Why joy again? Joy built trust, and from that we could build resilient communities. If anything, Paul said then, now should be the prime time for shared experiences in public spaces. Those words stayed with us because what Daily tous les jours does is build infrastructure for the human spirit.

As we navigate the challenges of the 21st century, from the ongoing effects of a social recession to the urgent need to address climate change, *The Joy Experiments* reminds us that joy isn't a luxury; it's a necessity. It's a force that can bind communities together, foster empathy, inspire positive change, and maybe even help us rethink capitalism. In a world that often feels divided, joy becomes a common language that unites people of diverse backgrounds, creating bridges where once there were walls.

The Joy Experiments is about the dimensions of life that reaffirm and nurture our humanity, qualities such as creativity, play, the stories we tell about who we are as a people and who we want to be, and the ability to imagine a collective future. In the hustle and bustle of our modern lives, it's easy to forget the power of joy. It feels as if we've been trained to dismiss joy as unproductive or inconsequential, relegating it to the realm of childhood. But joy is a necessity that requires adequate infrastructure.

As you embark on a journey through this book, we invite you to open your hearts, minds, and spirits to explore new possibilities and imagine what cities built for the human spirit can bring to our collective future.

Mouna Andraos and Melissa Mongiat
Daily tous les jours

Before You Begin

Good discussions often need periodic interjections of inspiration to keep them going. Since we hope a new kind of conversation comes about as a result of *The Joy Experiments*, we've done our best to feed you some of that inspiration in special direct conversations and comments from both of us, as well as in boxed sections sprinkled throughout the book. Our curiosity about what makes some cities so much more enthralling than others has led us into interesting corners and back alleys we'd like to take you to. Sometimes these boxes will explain a particular type of project that's resulted in creating a stronger sense of community. At other times, they'll outline how a city managed to stop organizing itself in the usual fashion long enough to see there can be new approaches to old problems.

We hope you treat these sections the way someone who every so often says, "That reminds me of something I once read," or "Here's something to consider." Those little side discussions always keep ideas and energy flowing.

A healthy discussion also requires a willingness to shift perspectives, so sometimes we provide an image of urban joy. Over the years, Paul has travelled far and wide with a camera and an eye for simple moments that have a way of uncovering the surprise, resilience, and everydayness of joy. We believe a new perspective often starts with looking differently at the things we never see.

Eventually, the boxed sections will take the shape of a podcast where we'll interview the people around the globe who are building the infrastructure for the human spirit and cities that will change the world.

Now join us in the journey.

INTRODUCTION

Because Cities Are Important

"Because cities are important" is the answer we give when people ask why HIP Developments invests in public activities that seemingly aren't connected at all to real estate, or why we personally spend so much time working with students, educators, artists, and anyone who shapes the personality of our community. Cities are special places. Mid-sized cities especially offer the scale that can tangibly influence the quality of our lives. At the same time, that scale is intimate enough for each of us to influence what our cities, and the whole world, can become in the future.

Having just tossed out a few bold statements, perhaps this is a good place to say a few words about Scott. Scott Higgins is a Canadian real estate developer and president of HIP Developments, which operates in Waterloo Region in Ontario, a collection of communities that's become a healthy tech hub successfully competing in the global innovation economy. Perhaps HIP is a good example of the opportunities and challenges that await many mid-sized cities in North America and the world. The company is part of that atmosphere of innovation and believes it plays a role in ensuring our communities evolve in step with the rapidly changing world around us.

HIP could simply drive maximum profit on its projects at all costs. But that approach ignores a very important and real fact: HIP's accomplishments are directly tied to the economic success and social health of Waterloo Region. If it chose to operate more broadly across Ontario, this ecosystem perspective would still apply. It would just be a bigger ecosystem. To view social, environmental, or political issues as completely disconnected from business is simply naive at best or wildly foolish at worst.

Another, and more personal, reason for Scott's thoughts on cities is that businesses are created and run by people. In the case of HIP, many of the employees, including Scott, were born in Waterloo Region and chose to stay and raise their families there. Scott had the opportunity to work in Toronto for one of the big banks but felt he had a chance to create real impact remaining in the region and supporting a dynamic mid-sized community. As for HIP, it isn't going anywhere. Waterloo Region is its home and primary market. We have no doubt that the return on investment and energy needed for city-building activity will be well worth it.

On top of all these reasons for participating in city building, there's also the well-documented fact that all of us have entered the Age of the City. As the world adapts to the digital revolution, the global economy, climate change, and other symptoms of massive disruption, cities rather than slow-moving national governments and organizations are the centre of the action. Cities have always been the hub of human invention. That won't change, and the output of those creative clusters will lead us to a better world.

Consider that approximately 100 cities are responsible for most of the economic, cultural, and innovative activity in the world, and that will only grow in the years ahead. The cities that invest in infrastructure that supports the inventive human spirit will succeed; the cities that don't will unquestionably fade.

Within this change toward supporting the human spirit, there's an opportunity for mid-sized cities. If these places can embrace this new mentality rather than solely focus on practical infrastructure needs, they can get a seat at the table of success. The more intimate aspect of mid-sized cities also gives them a chance to leap-frog some of the challenges of larger municipalities. However, this will take a commitment to embrace change through experimentation.

At this moment in time, the main difference between growth or decline will be the participation of citizens in shaping their cities. The responsibility doesn't rest exclusively with local governments or business leaders. It will come from the creative collaboration of all sectors and individuals.

Scott firmly believes Kitchener, Waterloo, Cambridge — Waterloo Region as a whole — can be one of those successful places. He also believes youth will be the yardstick of success. Will they be able to boldly change the world without leaving the community? Because of these beliefs, we're sharing our thoughts and the city-building experiments HIP is taking to create something other than real estate. Call it a manifesto of sorts or our "city-building workbook." The goal is to invite you to participate in our thoughts and activities whether you live in Waterloo Region; Champaign, Illinois; or somewhere in Germany. If we can turn mid-sized cities into the creative engines of the innovation economy, we'll have more solutions for the challenges we'll face in the future and we'll experience more joy.

During the Covid-19 crisis everyone discovered the reality that "we're all in this together." We should never lose this insight, especially at the city-building level. We are offering experiences in *The Joy Experiments* as a starting point for collaborative city building. We aren't saying what we did is what you should do, and we certainly aren't suggesting we know everything. We're sharing what we've done and what we've learned in the hope that it creates a common language and discussion among politicians, planners, citizens, and business leaders so we can create communities that contain the type of joy that fosters health, diversity, vibrancy, inventiveness, and economic success.

CHAPTER ONE

Under Attack

The Decline of the City Habitat

As a society, we've all become familiar with the concept that animals live in, and are supported by, habitats. We're finally discovering that sustainable habitats are a web of systems that interconnect and balance one another's impact on the overall ecosystem. These habitats can fall under attack when seemingly small facets of their surroundings are removed or damaged. Sadly, it's become clear that humans play a major role in that problem. With the belated gift of hindsight, we see the cascading negative effects inflicted on the environment because of our devotion to "progress." In 1885, Carl Benz invented the automobile with little knowledge or consideration to the side effects of fossil-fuel consumption and the air pollution that today threatens our climate. Back then, the world and its resources seemed infinitely large and we were naive. Today, we can no longer claim naïveté.

Now that we all know more about the patterns of cause and effect, we're taking action. We've cut out the use of pesticides on our lawns, we create sanctuaries to protect animals and plants, we buy from companies that plant trees with every purchase, and we protest, recycle, buy Teslas, and brake for turtle-crossing signs. Others simply choose to ride bikes to good bird-watching locations. We do this because we now understand the importance of protecting the habitat of the sugar maple, ruby-crowned kinglet, and the stunning emerald-shaded oil beetle, the bug that gives you blisters if you touch it but is still very cool to see. It's even cooler that we now care about it and all the other creatures great and small. Seventy years ago, we couldn't care less.

Let's hope society is coming to terms with these insights quickly enough to make a positive difference to the habitats of the life forms around us. But we, too, are life forms and depend on our habitats. We don't just mean clean air and water for our planet. In this book, we refer to social habitats such as neighbourhoods and cities. Cities are the infrastructure of our social needs and the source of the humanities (religion, art, politics, literature, philosophy, law, et cetera), invention, and collaborative cultures. Do we care about the interconnected web of factors that keep these habitats healthy so we can sustain the human spirit and our resilience? We've learned that the purple loosestrife plant, native to Europe, is an invasive species in North America and can quickly kill off wetland habitats. So we act in the hope of saving frogs, fish, salamanders, and birds. Do we work as vigorously to protect the structure of our cities to save the things that give us the things that feed our social soul?

We need to wake up and realize the social nature and fabric of our cities are under attack by at least two developments: the decline of progressive capitalism and the anti-social effects of social media and digital technology. Here's a conversation we had on these issues.

> **Cities are the natural habitat for the human spirit.**

Scott: It may sound odd for a real estate developer to say this, but I think capitalism has become brittle due to its dogmatic belief in infinite resources, the aggregation of wealth and power, and its almost religious tenet "greed is good." Clearly, it's a less-than-ideal platform for dealing with today's issues. Covid-19 has painfully illustrated that. Countries with more collaborative economic points of view acted on behalf of the collective good and overcame the challenges of the virus, while other nations, focused on the success of the individual, simply made things worse for all of their people.

While we feel these negative changes in a strong way today, capitalism didn't lose its way overnight. We've been warping and manipulating its value to society for a long time. Any economic system's greatest contribution is stability. In the past, capitalism warded off revolutions and the execution of kings by broadly distributing wealth. That didn't provide a uniformly even distribution, but it was broader than any efforts that came before. However, that distribution effort started getting bent out of shape sometime after the Second World War or thereabouts. At the beginning of the 20th century, products were often made, sold, and consumed within a community. But as the growing effects of the industrial era made themselves known, there was a drive for efficient mass production, and when that met up with cheap labour markets around the world, it was unstoppable. At times that change was small enough not to be noticed. But as we now know, it was a trend that shifted the economics of the world and altered the whole definition of what a community was and how it could support itself.

If I were to walk through the older urban parks of my city, I'd notice these spaces carry the same names as the early 20th-century industrial leadership of the community: Kaufman, Breithaupt, McCulloch, and Seagram. They weren't just the names of large and successful local businesses; they were also the names of local families. As a segment of society, these people felt a civic duty to help build the cities that supported their successes. That's a component of mid-sized-city culture that began to vanish as economies increasingly grew to global scales. For many cities, that sort of support simply doesn't exist anymore. Today, most company profits are exported to corporate head offices elsewhere, leaving cities without an active private-sector partner for social progress as more of the burden for urban improvement falls to the public sector and taxpayers. Local government politicians are painfully aware that we like to complain whenever our taxes go up, so there are very few options for finding replacements for that missing component of our habitat.

While the local philanthropic-funding issues affect social spaces such as parks and play areas, another trend — digital and social media platforms based on further efficiencies — is now transforming the physical and social patterns of our community interactions. This is being felt most acutely in the decimation of bricks-and-mortar retail, restaurants, and hospitality. These were the places we did the all-important act of "hanging out" with friends. Ask anyone who's been lonely for a long time and they'll tell you just how important "hanging out" is to mental health. This is a serious change to our habitat. The anti-social aspects of these technologies are pushing us headlong into a shift in the way we engage with our cities and one another.

Paul: Considering my former life as an executive at BlackBerry, it may also sound odd for me to wholeheartedly agree with Scott about the dangerous social effects of digital platforms. We all love our phones, but I don't like how human behaviour is being bent toward isolation and the impact it has on society's ability to experience the joy of collaboration, creation, and innovation. Those of us who were involved in the early days of the smartphone, just like Carl Benz and his automobile, had no idea what we were unleashing. There are days when I don't feel very good about what we created.

The largest impact of the digital age on our cities is in retail shopping. That may seem insignificant, but frankly it's not when you think about the role it's historically played in our social activities.

Every city in North America was partially built around the idea of a downtown that focused on retail commerce. Even small towns had their shopping and socializing main street. If Europe's idea of public activity involved cafés, coffee, and wine, North America's public space activity seems to have always been shopping. Today, mid-sized cities' downtowns have been crippled by suburban sprawl and the creation of shopping malls and big-box stores that cover the perimeters of these communities. The trajectory of this retail migration is a series of revolutions:

- **Retail 1.0:** The slow decline of owner-operator specialty stores and the creation of multi-offering department stores.
- **Retail 2.0:** The growth of national and international brands.

Ding!!
KA-CHING!!!

- **Retail 3.0:** The move toward suburban shopping malls and the subsequent decay of urban downtown cores.
- **Retail 4.0:** The proliferation of big-box stores.
- **Retail 5.0:** The demise of department stores and the hollowing out of shopping malls as online shopping becomes increasingly popular.

As stated above, these relentless revolutions have been driven by a primary objective — efficiency. With a promise of convenience, greater selection, and lower prices, the retail industry has worked to streamline all aspects of what consumers purchase and how they buy it. These revolutions have steadily aggregated distribution channels as well as physical and digital outlets. As we now move deeper into the world of e-commerce and the age of customer data, consumers themselves are being aggregated into the hands of a few online oligarchs such as Amazon, Expedia, and Walmart.

These new businesses don't just compete with existing retail outlets, they dominate and become category killers that eliminate all competition. They're an economic form of invasive species.

Paul: What we're witnessing is the altering of a key component of our city habitats. While these revolutions have delivered lower prices, they're also harming the social and economic structure of many small and mid-sized cities. Retail wasn't just about getting out of the house for instant gratification. Favourite stores got to know customers' names, likes, and dislikes. Conversations took place. These may be secondary contacts compared to family and friends, but research has shown these connections have a big impact on mental health. This isn't an insignificant issue when you consider the vast majority of North America's population resides in these mid-sized communities. We measure the economic value of efficiency but fail to link it to the measures of isolation, anxiety, and depression. Worse, no one feels they're accountable for the counter-effects of efficiency.

The retail revolutions also tell the story of the changing face of urban growth. With each stage of change, an area of a city and its infrastructure were abandoned for a new retail model and physical location. Downtowns and main streets were hollowed out as shopping malls began to cater to urban sprawl and the influence of the

The interconnected social fabric of cities supports collaboration, diversity, and invention.

automobile. Years later, these malls and department stores are now falling to the same fate as downtowns due to the introduction of big-box stores and e-commerce. With each stage, the concept of shopping as a public activity became more basic and less social while vast areas of our cities became undesirable. Adding to this struggle is the plight of restaurants and hospitality venues fighting to compete with SkipTheDishes and Uber Eats, which encourage people to stay at home and have led to the category-killer concept of the "ghost kitchen" — online restaurant brands that are delivery-only. Some ghost kitchens launch multiple online restaurants as they operate out of cheaper-rent warehouses. These threats and the effects of Covid-19 have generated a perfect-storm scenario in which close to 50 percent of bricks-and-mortar restaurants are expected to close in North America, while experts say ghost kitchens could grow to a $1 trillion industry by 2030.

Scott: These trends call into question what a city has to offer citizens in terms of social living. There's a desire among people to return to the city core, but what are they returning to? Online shopping is decimating the retail industry. Manhattan is worried about this trend, and if New York City is feeling the effects, then what chance does retail have of surviving in smaller communities?

These are the rather obvious effects of what I call "shitty capitalism." Paul says I can't trademark that phrase, but I'd like to try. Let's take a moment and discuss what we mean by shitty capitalism. The phrase is mine, but the basic fundamentals are actually widely acknowledged among economists and many forward-thinking business leaders.

Shitty Capitalism 101

THE WORLD SEEMS TO BE LIVING THROUGH A VERY DIFFICULT time of compounded change. Nothing works the way it should, or at least the way it used to. Our lives seem to get tighter as we fit into more confined roles. Meanwhile, other things are loose and fraying at the edges. More people need more than one job, and the concept of a career is becoming out of date for many. The cost of living is going up while confidence in the future goes down. Society is experiencing a much bigger shift than many of us realize. Capitalism has gone off its moorings and drifted away from how almost every sustainable system on this planet works.

One of capitalism's original goals was wealth creation and distribution by encouraging those who wanted to invent, build, and collaborate. It was a system, like nature, in which everyone in the "ecosystem" could play roles and to a certain extent be rewarded for ingenuity and effort. This allowed them also to become consumers of the system and distribute the wealth again. That sounds pretty good, right? Relatively fair, and, most importantly, sustainable.

A lot of that system still exists, but the big threat is the unbridled domination of a few who have a wealth-extraction ideology. It would be easy to blame pure greed by the 1 percent who have accumulated tremendous wealth and power. That's true, though shockingly it's more like 0.01 percent who have accrued most of the wealth. However, globalization and the massive tech monopolies are also contributing to this wealth-extraction trend.

We live in an ever-narrowing and archaic economic system that continually has wealth and opportunity extracted from it. Capitalism has become the engineered system for consumer debt, a form of capitalism that's turned shitty.

Does any sound person think this wealth-extraction ideology is sustainable? History and nature suggest not. If any one species in nature, such as an invasive plant, consumed all the nutrients in the soil, the whole ecosystem would fall apart. We know that, but when it comes to our own habitat we believe the model will somehow go on forever.

When we talk about the impact of shitty capitalism on cities and the need for fixing it, we're also speaking about a course correction for capitalism. If we can fix cities, perhaps we can fix the world.

Some people may worry we're recommending the overthrow of capitalism by socialism. We aren't. That feels like way too much work. We aren't thinking about socialism as a governing body or "state." It's more about capitalism having a bit of a heartbeat — "social capitalism." The idea here is to adopt a way of operating and commerce that values everyone. That's not suggesting everyone is treated the same or lives the same way, but that everyone has value. There are certainly things to learn from places such as Denmark. Contrary to what some might say, the Nordic countries aren't socialist states. They're capitalist nations that have an understanding that systems need to work under the same concepts as nature — the most durable and resilient system on the planet. §

Scott: A few years ago I visited Denmark with my family. My wife has relatives there who allowed us to experience the country, Copenhagen in particular, through the eyes of locals. It really is the best way to understand another culture. Through meals and long conversations on family sofas, I got a deep understanding about what it means to be Danish. The first thing I learned was how similar and different we were at the same time. We were similar in that people had careers, incomes, drive, and desires for a good life and good things. If I stopped at that description, you could say we were very similar. The difference wasn't in how Danes made their money but the way in which they spent it.

In Denmark, there's a belief that there should be a healthy balance between private spending and public good. In other words, an acknowledgement that life is played out in the public spaces of cities as well as in private homes, and the things that give us joy should be in both realms. This is a big shift from my experiences in North America. Our version of capitalism has led to the privatization of joy as we're encouraged to purchase ever-bigger TVs, pools, and home entertainment systems. However, in Copenhagen, there's an understanding that public spending is worth it if you can get joyful things to do in your city and they're free for anyone to use. It's almost as if each person manages a "joy budget" they use to fund private joy amenities as well as public joy amenities — things everyone experiences and shares as a community. Without question, their taxes are high, but the people I spoke to felt they got satisfaction from this form of allocation of their joy budget. They saw joy as part of their habitat.

I concluded that the big difference between my Danish friends and the world I live in isn't so much about the system of government or commerce as it is about the values of the people. They have a form of unwritten social contract that supports the idea that it's worth lifting everyone's quality of life through the use of amenities available to everyone — "we" amenities.

When I took my kids to see the sights of Copenhagen, I started to understand the Danish social contract as we experienced "we" amenities. There were free sidewalk trampolines in constant use by kids and adults alike along the Havengade. And there was the Round Tower, an old observatory that includes art exhibits and a beautiful library hall. Perhaps the most heartfelt experience we had was the simple bubble machine someone placed on the street and how a city was willing to slow down and enjoy it.

Don't blame the Danes' ability to be happy on being socialist. That's not the case. They just happen to understand that protecting their city habitats is worth it.

Urban magic time.

Other Ways Cities, Our Habitats, Are Under Attack

Businesses use efficiency to streamline actions, conserve effort, and heighten duplication, but that rarely fosters creativity that thrives within fractured effort, meandering thought, and the colliding of opposites. It's hardly surprising that over the years the uniqueness in the products and services we purchase has slowly disappeared. This is partially due to most of the national retail chains that have survived refusing to do business with small and mid-sized companies even when they offer innovative products. The "big boxers" prefer to deal only with large manufacturers that can scale to fit their market dominance and efficiency strategies. The result is that locally based start-ups are often blocked from effective distribution channels.

Meanwhile, the tech oligarchs who dominate our economy use their size and vendor application processes to search out competitors to copy or acquire. Not only does this limit healthy competition and our product choices, but it's also a perfect example of dominance out of control as it turns the fundamentals of capitalism on their head and marginalizes the health of local economies and entrepreneurial creative output.

Referencing cities as a human habitat that's complex and interconnected is part of a much bigger acknowledgement that nature can teach us a lot about strength and sustainability, even

Our social habitat is just as elaborate as that of nature. Destroying part of it, such as our downtown retail cores, has broad implications.

in economics and business. While much of the global economy focuses on the efficiencies of aggregation and compartmentalized decision-making, nature has always operated within a structure of dispersion and fragmentation because it makes ecosystems stronger, not weaker. Living systems function in networks that have layers of a few large units connected to millions of smaller ones, all with similar patterns, which allows them to withstand external threats better. Conversely, the streamlining of our economies in the name of efficiency can place us in states of vulnerability in which regional recessions can quickly become global. Disruption in supply chains can cascade shortages everywhere, while domination by a few business models can weaken an economic ecosystem to the point where it eventually even threatens the dominant businesses. To illustrate this point, there have been instances in which big-box stores, after entering a community with their low-wage/low-price business models, have found it difficult to maintain their operations because of the resulting community-wide job loss and reduction of wages.

The retail and digital revolutions are massive changes. Their impact on cities can't be fully comprehended yet, but it's clear that vibrant streets and social health are at stake. Local governments are challenged to address the problems because the problems include the fact that a great deal of the profits generated in cities don't stay there as they once did. Global companies don't invest in hometown firms. Instead, they extract wealth. As a result, cities are hit doubly hard with empty streets and a lower tax base with which to solve their problems.

We have to begin viewing cities as the smaller units in a living system network. If we start building cities differently, we can build economies differently. We can't continue to believe vibrant downtowns will simply happen using an old recipe. There's no logic that supports that thought. We need collaborative civic leadership that includes the private and public sectors. We need an appetite for experimentation. It's understandable that we all want to mitigate risk, but sometimes staying the same involves the biggest risk of all.

CHAPTER TWO

The Redesign of “We”

We hit you pretty hard in Chapter 1 with a list of problems in our cities that are contributing to the decline of social infrastructure and a resulting sense of a deeply divided society. So now we'd like to offer an optimistic observation. There's so much good in all of us, and humanity in general, that it makes one wonder why society is deeply divided at this time. History is full of stories showing the powerful good that can flow out of the human spirit. There are countless examples of communities and nations coming together when needed. And we've all experienced or heard stories of perfect strangers becoming friends once they find a common sports team or book they like. It seems to us that when there's the right kind of structure in place, humans as social animals are very good at getting along.

Scott: I don't think humanity is any different than it has ever been. What has changed is the shocking number of structures, products, and processes that have been designed to divide us. The problem with society is the communication tools we now rely upon and the environments in which we live. The difference between an optimistic future and a pessimistic one rests with how we change these environments, especially the most important environment of all — cities.

Both Paul and I have had the privilege of working with Bruce Mau, a brilliant mind, author of the book *Massive Change*, a global leader in design-led action, and a fan of the Joy Experiments. Bruce is a charismatic yet practical optimist about the future of the world, and when he talks about the changes we need to make in the world, he often states that if you close your eyes and then open them with a fresh view, 90 percent of what

you see will have been created by humans. So if we don't like the state of the world, we can redesign it because we designed it in the first place. That's a refreshing thought and quite accurate. The statement almost acts as permission to make things better — and I love that.

We have permission to redesign the things that are dividing us, and by doing that, we can redesign society, or as Paul and I like to say, we can redesign "we." When things are being built to divide us, we must construct more of the things that bring us together.

The redesign of "we" is important not just because of the issues we face today but also because of what the future holds in store. Tomorrow's challenges are the type that don't respect the traditional boundaries of our efficiency-oriented approaches to problem-solving. For example, the housing crisis that grips almost every city in North America has its roots in the widening gap between haves and have-nots, the globalization of our economy, the fact that our homes have become the primary investment vehicle for most citizens, and the not-in-my-backyard (NIMBY) movement. It's messy to say the least.

> **We must conceive new forms of infrastructure for the human spirit that will have the same positive social impact as corner stores and bowling alleys but are tailored for today.**

Solutions will require unprecedented negotiation and collaboration between all sectors and citizens. And when we add in the challenges associated with climate change, it's easy to assume we're quickly entering an era in which flexible thinking, dynamic planning, and united efforts at collaboration will be demanded of all of us. It will also be very important for everyone to experience tangible moments of shared joy, laughter, and a sense of being part of a community. These are the things that make the human spirit such a strong and sustainable force.

Cities, especially mid-sized ones, are the perfect place for redesigning "we" because they contain a scale that can tangibly change the quality of our lives while at the same time offering an intimacy that allows citizens the ability to influence what their communities can become. The journey toward that kind of hope starts with a renegotiation of the relationship between cities and citizens back to something that, in the past, was the foundation of a collaborative society.

In moments of difficulty, there's a natural desire for us to become nostalgic and view the past favourably. In the case of seeking a more connected and caring community, the past is a great place for inspiration. Many of us can imagine the socially vibrant communities from our childhood or movies that depict life in the 1930s, 1940s, or 1950s. Society might not have had everything right back then, but it absolutely had a lot of social infrastructure that gave people collective joy. It might not be possible to turn the clock back and put corner stores into every neighbourhood, however, the past, especially the North American story, can inspire us with far more than just simple examples of out-of-date social infrastructure. It also illustrates how we can successfully navigate the times we're in today.

Much of the social fabric from the first half of the 20th century was created in response to a time that was surprisingly similar to our current divisive society. In the book *Bowling Alone* by Robert Putnam, the author points out that America at the end of the 19th century was reeling from the negative effects of the Civil War, the Industrial Revolution, and massive waves of immigration in which people left all their communities, institutions, and traditions behind in their home countries and faced low-paying jobs and language barriers. All this led to high crime waves, the degradation of cities, inadequate education, and a widening gap between rich and poor that accelerated political corruption.

Hmm, that has a familiar ring to it.

North American society responded with a wave of civic enthusiasm that developed new forms of human spirit infrastructure that created what we now think of as "the good old days." This infrastructure included things such as churches, city squares, clubs, corner stores, pool halls, and even bowling alleys, hence the title of Putnam's book. Our nostalgic view of the past should include the story that there once was a time when city builders reprioritized infrastructure for the collective human spirit with the purpose of healing divided communities and building a strong and relatively united society.

The early 20th century was a real-life example of Bruce Mau's creed that if we don't like what's been designed, we can redesign it. So here's the good news — society has done this before and can do it again! We must reprioritize how we build cities and create new forms of infrastructure for the human spirit that will have the same moments of shared joy and positive social impact as corner stores and bowling alleys but are tailored for today.

This is a good moment for us to define what we mean when we use the word *joy*. After all, while being a very short word, it contains a tremendous amount of emotion and can have several applications. When we started relating the word to the city-building projects HIP Developments was working on, we utilized it as the emotional opposite of other words employed to describe many North American mid-sized cities, such as *predictable*, *dull*, and *grey*. But we've continued to learn that joy has far more value than being audaciously attention-getting.

In the book *The Timeless Way of Building*, a sort of bible for architects and city planners, author Christopher Alexander struggles to find a suitable word to describe a certain quality that connects buildings and spaces to our humanness. With dissatisfaction, he works his way through words such as *comfortable*, *alive*, *egoless*, and many others. We've added to that list the word *joy* and feel it's very relevant for the times we live in. For us, joy is something people experience when they're linked to others or to something beyond themselves. In fact, joy is something people most often feel when they're released from self-absorption, when they're caught up in everything that's around them and forget issues and personal judgments.

Joy in action on a small and personal scale can inject quality into the fabric of our cities and involves the renegotiation of our social perspectives and the alteration of our infrastructure. A good example of that effort can be seen at the Working Centre in Kitchener, Ontario. This organization was created by Stephanie and Joe Mancini in 1982 to respond to unemployment and poverty in the downtown core of that city. The organization is well known for helping those in need of food, shelter, housing, training, social enterprise, jobs, and even help doing their income taxes. And that's a very incomplete list of what it does.

We met with Joe to discuss the importance of joy at the Working Centre because so many people told us he was an important stop on our journey. Our expectation was that we'd hear about inserting moments of music or games into the tasks of delivering food or counselling — the equivalent of corporate team-building exercises only for the disadvantaged. But what we learned was something quite different.

A good place for starting to understand the uniqueness of the Working Centre is this quote from the book *Transition to Common Work*, written by Joe and Stephanie: "The Working Centre is best experienced with your feet on the ground, feeling the vibrancy of its spaces and places, watching how ideas and practices live in the midst of a community at work."

What a fascinating phrase to use — "community at work." It's basically the opposite of what many of us feel in society today. That sense of community hits you quickly when you enter the primary building operated by the Working Centre. It's not accurate to call the room a lobby; it's a public space where a diverse group of people with various needs interact with one another. Some work through serious problems while others just talk to each other. It's the antithesis of any waiting room we've ever been in.

A conversation with Joe always circles back to this idea of a community at work. It's easy to assume that the products of the Working Centre are things like food and shelter, but in Joe's mind the most important one is a real community and the joy that can be found within it. In fact, that joy is what has sustained Stephanie and Joe's commitment to their undertaking for more than 40 years.

The first days of the Working Centre were a response to the early 1980s economic downturn caused partially by a push toward globalization and a battle against inflation that delivered the crushing weight of high interest rates on those who could withstand them the least. It was a combination that resulted in the thinning out of the working class. Looking back, it's easy to see that this was the start of a long evolution and splintering of our economic system toward a structure that today offers less to more and more people.

Joe spoke about the obvious needs of food and shelter at this time but also about a greater issue that, left unchecked, had the potential to cause long-lasting negative effects within society. As he told us, "People were experiencing

> **The future will be joyful or we won't have one.**
> **— Bruce Mau**

the double frustration of feeling that work was withheld from them and that their empty pockets limited their participation in society."

The people the Working Centre served were the first wave coming out of the postwar years to feel the social isolation and loneliness that's rampant today. People had to feel they were part of a community and had purpose as much as they needed the basics. Without that sense of collaborative purpose and joy, there was little hope of breaking out of a cycle of despair.

Stephanie and Joe performed a type of renegotiation by turning the economic and social norms causing the problems upside down. They prioritized the idea of producing things that helped others over personal acquisition and society's fixation on individual gratification. The concept of "work" was redefined from being a task to being viewed as a gift that connected people to meaningful purpose and their community. The Working Centre wasn't a complete rejection of capitalism; it offered a reprioritization within that system, in which doing and collaborating were more important than acquiring and competing.

As an example, people weren't just invited to eat nutritious meals but also to help make them, serve them, and clean up afterward. An integrated community took shape as buildings were purchased and renovated, supportive housing projects evolved, social enterprises such as cafés and thrift stores created useful and interesting places, and a sizable market garden added beauty. Today, it's sometimes hard to know who's a paid employee, volunteer, or recipient of the Working Centre's services. That's because some people belong to more than one of these categories.

In our conversation with Joe, he remained emphatic that more joy and connection can be experienced at the Working Centre than in many more affluent sectors of society. The Working Centre example also illustrates an important point about how we as a society reach the objective of joy. It's not just about adding a new goal to our status quo processes. It requires us to ask new questions, turn things upside down, reshuffle the deck, and throw a few friendly wrenches into the works. All this makes us think about a profound statement that Bruce Mau made at a conference devoted to the Joy Experiments. His clear and eloquent message to us was: "The future will be joyful or we won't have one." The Working Centre lessons underline this phrase and add this insight: joy is also the way to get to the future.

Think about that for a moment: creating collective joy along the way to the future will make us far more resilient and productive than our current environment of distrust and loneliness will.

The Joy Experiments offer a model for examining our problems and opportunities differently and prioritizing infrastructures that bring us together, ones in which the human spirit can create moments of collective joy. This joy model can be applied to many of our most important issues with meaningful outcomes. For example:

- **Joy can boost the economy:** Today's economy runs on ideas, invention, and the people who create them. A city's ability to attract creative talent through vibrant living, collaborative spaces, and a lifestyle that blends work and play will determine its economic future.
- **Joy can make housing more affordable — and fun:** Joyful cities redefine what it means to live in a "smaller" house by devoting urban public space to playful participation. In this model, neighbourhoods are the best amenity for a home or condominium. The city becomes everyone's communal backyard.
- **Joy can make inclusiveness possible:** As much as cities strive for inclusiveness, the reality is that money usually gets in the way. The true metric for determining inclusivity and quality of life is how much joy can be experienced in a city for free.
- **Joy can improve mental health:** Joyful cities prioritize the need for social connection and positivity that comes out of collaborative moments of play. In these moments, strangers become neighbours. Shared ideas become invention and the engines of prosperity.
- **Joy reduces political and social division:** Joyful cities create more united citizens by moving people out of seclusion and into collaboration. Unity and a collective vision for the future also facilitate experimentation, since citizens are more willing to allocate tax dollars to projects that create collective value.

When joy is prioritized as a city-building objective, it becomes the key to creating a future in which the human spirit does more than survive — it thrives.

Joe Mancini puts a very human face to the power of the joy model. He chooses to tackle some of the most difficult and chronic problems in society, yet always seems to be smiling. Joe's a very happy person. To paraphrase a lyric by Canadian singer-songwriter Bruce Cockburn, Joe and Stephanie seem to kick at the darkness till it bleeds joy. Make no mistake: joy is the best form of activism!

Art and real life become one.

CHAPTER THREE

Starting the Journey

American stand-up comedian and recording artist Lord Buckley once said: "They didn't know where they was going, but they knew where they was … wasn't it." That's an apt commentary when considering the plight of many of today's cities, especially Detroit.

Paul: A few years before I started collaborating with Scott, I went to Detroit to shoot an experimental photo essay of that city and its now-famous struggles. I hired a guide to take me into the heart of the city's darkness. I think he carried a gun, and for some bizarre reason, I found that comforting. What I saw was a city and people who were abandoned and held in disregard because it was easier to just pick up and move away rather than stay and adapt the city for the future.

First, the factories left for larger and cheaper spaces and took the city's tax base with them. Then the people who could afford to move followed. What was left was a ghost town full of ghosts. People who viewed my photos would ask if they were from some war-torn country far away. Of course, their jaws dropped when I told them they were looking at scenes only three hours away.

As shocking as Detroit was and still is, there's nothing overly unique about it. Detroit is just the ultimate example of what the Western world has been doing for several hundred years — treating resources as if they were unlimited and always heading for the horizon when there was no longer enough "good life" to go around.

That experience got me thinking about the changing world around me and how it was getting smaller and more challenging. Where do we go when there's no longer a frontier, when there are no unlimited resources beyond the horizon? It seemed to me that if the answer was no longer

CITY HALL
SCHO

As we run out of unlimited resources and endless horizons to move beyond, the frontier becomes our cities and human inventiveness.

"over the next hill," then the frontier had to be within our cities and the unlimited resource of human inventiveness. Disregard would have to be replaced with regard for others.

Detroit illustrated both the problem and the solution. While the devastation was breathtaking, there was also a surprising human defiance against the odds that revealed itself in expressive public art, historical pride, cool restaurants, slow-roll bike rides, and a few bold new businesses that understood the importance of their connection to the local social fabric that brought communities together. There were aspects of that part of Detroit I wished I could bring back home with me. Detroit represented a new idea — "the frontier within."

When Scott and I met, it was as if we'd metaphorically wandered down different streets but ended up standing on the same corner. We didn't care when the light changed — we were crossing anyway, because we firmly believed the time had come for a new approach to city building. The world had already changed drastically, and we needed to catch up. Businesses and markets had become global, and despite all the debates on that topic, there was really no going back. The tech industry continued to be absorbed into a small handful of Goliath-like companies that operated everywhere and acted as if they had accountabilities nowhere. All this changed the purpose and context in which cities existed.

The Slow Roll to Joy

WE LIKE TO HIGHLIGHT ACTIVITIES AND PROJECTS IN OTHER places that we feel align with our Joy Experiments. Perhaps someday we'll hand out Joy Experiment Achievement Awards. If we do, Slow Roll in Detroit will be one of the first recipients.

Mike MacKool and Jason Hall started Slow Roll as a simple bike ride among friends in Detroit with only one real rule: anyone could join if they wanted to. If you've ever been to Detroit, you'll know that many of the old downtown neighbourhoods have wide four-lane roads, and in the city's current state of abandonment, they're mainly empty of traffic. In that respect, Detroit is the perfect place to ride a bike. The Monday night bike rides grew in popularity, and at some point in that growth process, MacKool and Hall noticed that people of every colour and from every community had joined in the rides with smiles on their faces. That insight led MacKool and Hall to turn Slow Roll into a well-executed city-building exercise. More than 3,000 people joined the weekly rides through different Detroit neighbourhoods. In a city perceived to be on its knees, people began to feel they could do something they could take pride in — pride in themselves and pride in their city.

There are a lot of barriers in Detroit, social as well as physical ones, such as freeways, strip malls, and walled neighbourhoods. Slow Roll allowed people to get out of their part of Detroit, slow down, see the city for what it truly is, and experience what's on the other side of freeways. Black teens on low-riders, hipsters on fixies, and families from the suburbs all rode together, and their Slow Roll chant was a source of resilience and city pride. It's an example of what the human spirit can do when it steps away from the virtual digital world and does something tactile and collective. As a result of Slow Roll, Detroit created and celebrated stories about the city. In fact, people have moved to Detroit because of Slow Roll.

Paul's experience in Detroit and the Slow Roll story was so moving for him that he's now the proud owner of a Detroit Bike A-Type bicycle. Detroit Bikes is the only large-scale bike-frame factory in the United States. Its owner, Zakary Pashak, founded the company because he realized there were a lot of skilled unemployed workers in Detroit who knew how to bend steel. If you want to discover what kind of impact those bikes have had on the workforce, watch the Henry Ford II video at michiganbicyclelaw.com/henry-ford-ii.

It's all joy, pure and simple. §

Cities used to say they were the "home and birthplace of Company X." Today, cities compete against one another for small slices of companies. That approach brings some jobs, but the profits that once helped fund city parks and social causes are now funnelled to the cities that house head offices.

On the surface, it would seem cities are hopelessly on the losing end of globalization except for one thing: *ideas!* Cities have always been the engines of new ideas and innovation because they offer the scale, density, and infrastructure for people to meet, collaborate, and inspire one another. To quote the book *Happy City* by Charles Montgomery, "The most important physiological effect of a city is the way in which it moderates our relationship with other people." There was a time when cities in North America prospered or declined based on whether railways ran through them. We have a theory, based on all we've read and witnessed in other cities, that today's version of the railway is human talent and creativity. Many cities understand this dynamic and have invested heavily in infrastructure for the human spirit. As a result, they're playing a very important and valued role in the new world we're moving into. These are the cities that hold the promise of being home to the next "big thing" because they're also home to joy. The people who live in these places have great civic pride because the city respects the human needs of their citizens. They're creating a much-needed balance of power in the global economy. They give globalization roots, and in doing so, give all of us some form of self-determination in this new world.

So we believe that *localism matters because globalism matters.*

That's the context for our efforts and our Joy Experiments. We aren't just looking for ways to make our community more fun or cooler. Our experiments aren't exercises in applying wallpaper or veneer to drab back alleys. Joy Experiments are an exploration on how to make our communities, and cities of similar size and makeup, more sustainably prosperous and livable in the global economy. When we started out, we listed a series of issues we felt needed to be the focus in our work if we hoped to build infrastructure for human spirit in Waterloo Region.

The list of issues isn't complete, since we're sure there are more and certainly each community is unique. But the list we offer here will give you a sense of the surprising breadth of factors that can affect the resilience of a city. We tackled some of the issues with solid tactics while others were addressed with strategies that are very much works in progress. Our hope is that through experimentation we can turn these topics into the infrastructure that instills joy that leads to civic energy, innovation, and sustainable prosperity.

The issues you'll see time and again in this book are as follows.

IDENTITY

There are a lot of different words that could be used to describe how citizens think about themselves and their city: *image, culture, brand.* But we like *identity.* Everyone completely understands the identity issue at the national level.

Canadians endlessly debate and wonder what our identity is or what it means to be Canadian. Few ask that question when it comes to mid-sized cities.

Identity, or culture, is the collection of stories we tell about ourselves and how we celebrate those stories. That might not seem all that important, but here's the interesting part: you attract what you celebrate. The stories we tell about our cities set the course for their future.

Stories can be inclusive and exclusive. Cities need to take active accountability for the curation of their stories to ensure they're positive for everyone in the community.

CREATIVITY

Creativity isn't exclusive to the arts or any other segment of society. It's not a "thing," like a painting or a song. *It's what our minds and imaginations* do *when we're trying to make something that doesn't yet exist or when we want to solve a problem.* And we're all capable of being creative to one degree or another. Why is that important to city building? As discussed earlier, innovation, ideas, and invention are the most important outputs of city life, and their value will only increase in the future.

Second, city building itself is a creative activity. Most of what we discuss in this book isn't necessarily new, but we've done a great deal of reimagining to explore different outcomes. It's not quite a magic trick, but it is creative.

Finally, as you'll see in subsequent chapters, we feel problem-solving creativity is a big part of the Waterloo Region story past and present. And we believe it needs to be part of our future, as well.

YOUTH

Here's one truth about cities: they start to die when young people feel they need to move away to follow their dreams. There are towns all over the country in decline because they've lost the next homegrown generation of dreamers.

There are many measurements for success for city building, but our youth is the one that matters most. Kids from all aspects of our cities need to feel they have a future in their hometowns or they'll be attracted to the cities that offer it.

COLLABORATION

As national governments respond slowly and rigidly to the changing winds of globalization, cities are adapting quickly and rising in power by creating new forms of collaboration involving the public, private, and educational sectors. Places such as Indianapolis, Austin, Copenhagen, and Waterloo Region have given their communities economic focus and prosperity by combining the knowledge of world-class educational and research institutions with the inventiveness of the private sector and support from the public sector. *When knowledge and resources cross old barriers within our communities, they can change everything.*

TALENT ATTRACTION

If cities are the source of invention and innovation, then making them appeal to talented and creative people is critical. Innovative minds like to blur the lines between work, social, and play. When you think of the old coffee houses of Vienna, or the bars and factory lofts of SoHo in New York City, it's clear creative people have always thrived on conversation, collaboration, and interesting experiences.

Talent creates ideas and money follows them. The economic success of cities is directly linked to the type of social environment they can offer the public.

PUBLIC SPACES

Ken Greenberg, an internationally known city planner from Toronto, once said you can judge how livable a city is by how much you can do without spending any money. That's an interesting benchmark for determining how vibrant a city should be. In Europe, this is a given. Public squares are full of people, and all that's required are a few tables, chairs, and coffee. However, in North America, we're less comfortable hanging out in public without a scheduled purpose. But that, too, is changing. *We're learning we need physical spaces that define our community and allow us to step outside our social media silos, meet strangers, and play ... for free.* Public spaces are the front lines of countering the divides in our society.

SELF-DETERMINATION

Throughout this book, we make the argument that the purpose and role of cities have changed, and to keep up we need a different style of planning and public participation. That will also require a different style of leadership, both public and private.

In terms of politics, sound fiscal planning and the looking after of current needs are quickly becoming basic requirements. They're very much needed but won't makes cities more competitive. *A new type of leadership is required at the local level, one that goes beyond fundamental decision-making to inspire citizens to want a great city rather than a "good enough" one.* We require local "Winston Churchills" who have the qualities to motivate large groups of people to action. This will be critical because identity, celebration, and quality of life need to be applied to all citizens, which means everyone should be able to participate in the advancement of these issues ... especially quality of life.

In turn, the private sector must expand its commitment to the city ecosystems from which it profits. There was a time when private-sector money built parks and hospitals for the benefit of workers. If talent and ideas are the fuel of future success and cities are the engine, then we must have leadership from all sectors helping to drive change.

The above issues and themes are the battlefields on which we've chosen to experiment with and shift thinking from seeing joy as frivolous to being needed and practical.

Playing in public.

CHAPTER FOUR

Bring Your Own City

Sometimes it seems a small event can grow into what big thinkers such as Bruce Mau call "massive change." Those small changes are often referred to as the butterfly effect, which explains how the path of a tornado can be influenced by minor disruptions such as the flapping of the wings of a distant butterfly several weeks earlier.

As we wrote *The Joy Experiments*, the world was living through the effects of the first two waves of Covid-19. It will take a lifetime for us to fully comprehend what changes the pandemic has thrust upon us. One thing is certain: some things will change and many more, surprisingly, won't. Human nature will remain human nature. We'll continue to be social creatures and still pursue happiness and joy. That's now clear as Covid has become a lesser concern for many people. Most of us are travelling again, attending our favourite sports and performing arts events once more, and not wearing masks these days.

Some people have predicted that Covid-19 is the first step in the demise of big cities. However, the long-term global view suggests there will continue to be a large-scale immigration to urban areas. The expectation is that by 2050 two out of every three people in the world will be living in cities.

Even in the midst of the first Covid-19 wave, many people were unable to quickly evacuate to second homes. In many instances, these people became shining examples of resilience and innovation. They showed how overlooked spaces could become surprising places of vibrancy and took it upon themselves to reimagine

what "community" could be. They remained, endured, and demonstrated why cities are the source of our humanity. So, rather than witnessing the death of cities, perhaps we're seeing the start of a great rebirth.

But among all these events is there a butterfly effect?

Well, one reaction to Covid-19 that quickly became a reality for nearly everyone was the work-from-home adjustment. Zoom and other online meeting platforms made this shift much easier. The tech industry, which was already comfortable with teams of workers around the world, took this change in stride and publicly stated it might never return to office life again. Many organizations calculated the benefits of lower overhead costs and saw the potential for a positive impact on their bottom lines.

It's hard to know how big this work-from-home trend will be, but it isn't going away. Even if it ends up only affecting 20 percent of the workforce, that will still cause huge shifts in society, influencing everything from home designs to the sales of sweatpants. Working from home could be the faraway flap of a butterfly wing that turns the competitive landscape of cities upside down.

Paul: While I watched society's descent into the 2020 Covid-19 spring lockdown, I was captivated with how smoothly we shifted to digital-meeting connections. Sure, there were the "Larry, you're on mute ... we can't hear you" moments, but all things considered, business made changes everyone previously thought would have taken years to implement. There's a Nelson Mandela saying, "It's always impossible — until it's done." That's a fundamental truth about life, and I think it also applies to the work-from-home phenomenon.

As the subject of conversations transitioned to working from home becoming permanent, I couldn't help but think this was part of a much longer trend I had experienced in my days at Research In Motion (RIM), the creators of the BlackBerry. Back then, we experienced the *consumerization* of the enterprise, which referred to the slow but steady growth of more consumer-oriented tech tools in offices by employees. The first example of this was the laptop with user-friendly interfaces and the freedom of not being chained to a desktop and a green screen. It was the initial step for work going home and home going to work. When cellphones and later smartphones arrived, companies bought them for their employees. For many years, BlackBerrys weren't sold to individuals but to IT departments that then handed them out to their employees. BlackBerry scaled its company to this distribution model and became a runaway success.

Then Apple launched the iPhone to target consumers, and though people loved the simple and fun user experience, RIM didn't think it was a threat to the BlackBerry, since its device was a serious business tool based on security. Over time, workers didn't want the complications of two phones — work and personal — and started complaining that the personal phone was far easier to use, so why couldn't the work phone operate like the iPhone? They wondered: Why can't workers just have one phone and why can't it be metallic rose?

Soon, the issues of security were easily solved through third-party software applications, and IT managers became tired of trying to be order takers for a variety of different smartphones. Their solution was to say, "Go buy any phone you want as long as it can support our company's security needs and submit the bill as an expense." This became known as "bring your own device" (BYOD) and led to a landscape change that BlackBerry was never able to adjust to. The IT people RIM dealt with said, "Don't talk to me. Go talk to all our staff." Basically, we weren't able to fully comprehend or deliver the things consumers wanted in a smartphone.

BYOD had much broader and more cultural implications than kicking off the demise of the BlackBerry. With iPhones and MacBooks in hand, the definition of an office changed to include places like the local Starbucks. BYOD was overtaken by the next logical step in the consumerization of the enterprise — bring your own office (BYOO). Now, it seems to me, we're on the verge of bring your own city (BYOC). In this scenario, companies don't care what city employees choose to live in. As a result, BYOC could have a massive impact on how cities normally attract jobs and create economic prosperity.

Bring your own city (BYOC) ushers in a new era in which cities that create joy win.

Traditionally, cities create jobs by attracting businesses. In every city hall, there's an economic development department, one of whose tasks is to target and pitch to companies the benefits of relocating or setting up new offices in its city. Such departments espouse the benefits of reliable infrastructure like roads, sewers, hospitals, airports, and perhaps local educational institutions. They knock on the doors of executive suites all over the globe and sweeten the pot with tax incentives. But in the BYOC era, the response from the decision-makers may eventually become "Don't talk to me. Go talk to all our staff. We don't care where they work." In the flap of a butterfly wing, the value proposition that assures a city's growth could be flipped on its head. Roads, sewers, and tax incentives may take a back seat to cities with vibrant streets, a strong sense of community, fairness in housing, and the ability to provide individuals with *joy*!

BYOC doesn't assume every employee will have the freedom to work wherever they want. The ones who are asked to work in offices may be a select group of employees who are the innovators and collaborators. The role of office spaces may transform into the sharing of ideas and the spark of creativity. Companies will want to place those creative clusters in environments that offer more stimulation. So consider BYOC as a juxtaposition in workspaces. Some people will work from home in whatever city they want, while others will work in increasingly funky commercial office buildings presented as artifacts of company culture near sources of knowledge, finance, and creative stimuli.

To illustrate this point, in the heart of the 2020 Covid-19 pandemic, while everyone was predicting an exodus from New York City, Apple, Amazon, and Facebook acquired more than 148,000 square metres of office space. Rather than implementing work-from-home master plans, these companies shifted to have enough new office space to hire 15,000 more employees in that city. Even smaller companies understood there was value in only partial-work-from-home edicts. In an October 2020 *New York Times* article, Dev Ittycheria, the chief executive of MongoDB, a cloud database platform whose headquarters are in Midtown Manhattan, said, "We believe that being physically present with colleagues in an office can offer important opportunities for in-person interaction, collaboration, and connection that are important for the success of our company."

Scott: Ironically, scenarios for both work from home and creative-cluster workspaces will require cities to view joy as one of their key economic value propositions. Many cities are already heading in this direction with big investments in exciting and surprisingly engaging urban parks. These spaces are inspired more by Disney than baseball fields and swing sets. Boston's Rose Kennedy Greenway contains sculpture fountains, a hand-carved carousel, zip lines, beer and wine gardens, and outdoor yoga surfaces.

A powerful advance in Toronto is the Daniels Waterfront area, also called "City of the Arts." It's not park space; it involves creative spaces designed to bring innovative thinkers, business, education, and ideas together into what I call a very free-flowing community of creativity. The area is home to George Brown College, OCAD University, Artscape, architectural and legal firms, and even a bank. Everything about it, from architecture to interiors and even its location, was thoughtfully designed to foster creativity, collaboration, and invention among students and the business community that surrounds it. The schools don't have lecture halls and traditional classrooms. Instead, the key features are hands-on collaborative workspaces and labs that encourage students and industry partners to push the boundaries of design. Artscape has used this area to give birth to a self-sustaining social enterprise called Launchpad, which brings creative minds together under one roof in a highly collaborative and multidisciplinary environment. Its goal is to connect people with business opportunities and resources. I admit I get excited by the leadership demonstrated within these examples.

A lot of people are considering the work-from-home model to be the death of big cities and an easy win for smaller centres that can offer a lower cost of living. I believe that to be an oversimplification. Creativity and invention will continue to be the drivers of economic growth. People, with a choice of where to live, will demand more out of their community. We aren't witnessing the death of big cities; we're seeing the growing power of vibrant cities of all sizes.

There will be winners and losers in this trend, as with all trends. Winning will require a bolder form of civic leadership than we've had in the past. When you combine the effects of BYOC with the massive decline in bricks-and-mortar retail

City streets carry us away.

Even office space will be designed to foster creative thought.

(which we touched on in Chapter 1), a prosperous urban centre will require a different collaborative leadership model that affords a willingness for experimentation.

Currently, experimentation is a very infrequent strategy at the civic level. For about the past 40 years, there's been a rather consistent trajectory of prosperity and an assumption of growth for many mid-sized cities. Some large cities have faced an urban-decay crisis and there have been economic ups and downs, but for the most part, cities grew in tandem with the prosperity of Western society. The status quo was good and the desire for bold and disruptive vision waned. "Visionary" slowly stopped being a job skill listed on the resumés of mayors and city councilmembers. It was replaced with descriptors such as "sound fiscal responsibility" and "a steady hand at the wheel." Without a perceived need for change, the objective of municipal governments became finding more efficient ways of keeping things the same. One could even say there was a strong shift to fulfill the desires of citizen groups seeking lower taxes. To be clear, there's nothing wrong with what we've just described when times are good and there's no threat to the status quo and no disruptive competition. But as has already been suggested, those days have come to an end. The ingredients of city building are changing, and the competition between cities has become more intense. Much has been written about how to build healthier, sustainable, vibrant cities, and there certainly are civic officials who know what they need to achieve. However, they still operate in structural models that are risk-averse and strive to have full control over the outcome of their initiatives prior to taking steps forward. The result is that many innovative ideas simply get stuck in a machine that was, quite frankly, built for another time. Some mid-sized cities falsely believe they can set their own timetable and grind away at trying to achieve new things using old processes.

Scott: A perfect illustration of this "good things get stuck" model and the alternative approach in which collaboration between the private, public, and institutional sectors can embrace experimentation and "unstick" innovative city-building ideas is the story of how Paul and I met and began working together.

Paul: In 2016, I was asked by Waterloo Region's Creative Enterprise Initiative (CEI) to develop a strategy for attracting world-class innovation economy talent to the area through the use of vibrant public spaces. I wasn't hired because I had vast amounts of public space design experience but rather due to an ability to wrap my brain around vague abstract thoughts and craft well-articulated strategies. It also helped that in my previous career I'd visited many of the communities Waterloo Region competes against. For the CEI project, I researched and visited places such as Quartier des spectacles in Montreal where ways were found to joyfully celebrate the world-class activity that had been hidden behind doors and walls in very public ways. Some of the key things I learned were that communities attract what they celebrate and what they don't celebrate they slowly lose. I concluded that Waterloo Region had always been a community of makers and innovators, but a humbleness had always prevented the area from being great storytellers. With a growing need for world-class talent, the time had come to not only be makers and innovators but also to become *celebrators*.

My strategic report, *Creative Intersections*, was delivered to CEI and its key stakeholders, including the Region of Waterloo. In a nutshell, "Creative Intersections" involved taking some of the ideas and content conceived within many of the region's world-class organizations and giving them to installation artists to reinterpret and fill public spaces with engaging and fun art. Through this approach, public spaces would be able to tell the stories of what Waterloo Region was and what it could become in the future. While the report was extremely well received, my gut assumption was that the vision was far too bold for the local government to act upon alone. It needed private-sector collaboration, an insight that was written right into the document. That was one of the reasons the report was called *Creative Intersections*. My hope was that the regional government would at least champion the idea and start exploring those collaborative partnerships.

Bluntly put, that didn't happen. It simply got stuck. However, there's another unique characteristic within the region I'd underestimated — a hands-on collaborative attitude often led by the private sector. Some call it a barn-raising approach, acknowledging the community's Mennonite heritage, but it's really all about city building. It's the bold collaborative attitude that brought the University of Waterloo into being, and much to my surprise, would breathe new life into the "Creative Intersection" strategy.

Scott: Within the "Creative Intersections" strategy, Paul had offered up some examples of how local business innovations, in the hands of public artists, could animate the Grand River in downtown Cambridge. When I was given the report by local architect and business leader Roger Farwell, I was in the middle of conceiving a large European-type public square as part of the Gaslight District real estate project HIP was building in the area. "Creative Intersections" gave me the framework to not only develop engaging spaces but to also start collaborative efforts between the city, the University of Waterloo's School of Architecture, the Grand River Conservation Authority, and HIP. Paul and I developed a "Creative Intersections" that celebrated the region's Grand River. Early promotion of the Gaslight District unquestionably demonstrated there was a strong appetite among

[**Efficient sameness won't get us where we need to go.**]

citizens for exciting urban spaces in Cambridge. With our new "Creative Intersections" concept, I approached the City of Cambridge with an unorthodox idea — an urban park with playful yet meaningful art, event halls, a public square, and cafés. It was an idea that would require an equally unusual partnership with the city.

The usual path to building a condo project such as the Gaslight District would involve giving city hall a cheque for something termed "cash in lieu of parkland." In this case, the amount was $1.5 million, which would usually go to fund arenas, baseball diamonds, and other conventional infrastructure around the city. But we knew the City of Cambridge had a strong need to revitalize its downtown core, and we had a vision for a different kind of park — a vibrant urban one. Usually, we'd ask for an "unconventional allocation" so we could direct those funds to our project. And usually the answer, regardless of the city involved, would be no. I'd been down this road before and knew I needed to shuffle the deck if I wanted a *yes!*

I decided to approach Doug Craig, the mayor at the time, with an invitation to experiment together. Cambridge needed vibrant place-making to save its downtown, and conventional infrastructure wouldn't get people playing and staying in the urban core. What was needed was an investment in joy. Doug knew me well enough to be prepared for surprises when I walked into his office, and I didn't disappoint him. I laid out our "Creative Intersections" plans and told him we were prepared to double our cash in lieu of parkland investment to make it happen. Would he allow our required payment to go toward this urban park? Would he experiment in joy with us? Financially, it would be our roll of the dice. Mayor Craig agreed to collaborate, and so did Gary Dyke, his chief administrative officer.

Today, as a result of this bold discussion, Cambridge is home to the world's largest living architecture sculpture, *Meander,* created by Philip Beesley, a School of Architecture faculty member. The work is inspired by *our* Grand River and offers insight into nature's resilience, sustainability, and diversity. You'll learn more about *Meander* and its impact on cultural identity and city building in ensuing chapters.

Kathryn McGarry, the next mayor, was also supportive of this collaborative partnership. The impact of *Meander* has shown the power of unconventional thinking, and Mayor McGarry has established a $35 million core transformation fund that has urban place-making and joy as objectives. It's a good example of how private and public sectors can work together and how the former can take risks. Once these ideas are experienced by the population, they're enjoyed and become mainstream, making it easier for levels of government to instigate similar projects on a more regular basis.

The model of full collaboration between private, public, and institutional sectors is the path to city building for our times. It's not the exclusive job of the mayor and city council. It involves everyone, and as a result, it can circumvent the old management models whose objectives were efficient sameness. Being on the winning side of the BYOC trend will require different city-building game plans that set out to achieve different goals such as creating civic joy. It's not impossible, just different.

City of Murals

TO DATE, MURAL ARTS PHILADELPHIA HAS CREATED MORE THAN 3,600 murals in its city. That's an unbelievable number if all you wanted to do was cover up unsightly walls and brighten a neighbourhood with a splash of colour. In fact, if that was Mural Arts Philadelphia's primary goal, chances are it would have never been done. Somewhere along the way, probably after 50 murals, it would have run out of energy, ideas, and happy flower themes. But Philadelphia had a deeper purpose than that. These murals are a tool to unite communities and visually tell the stories that say "This is us … coming together in mutual respect … 3,600 times."

For this organization and the city, murals aren't nearly as important as the process that creates them, because what they're really working to achieve is "Change for the Better" at community and individual levels.

The process for each mural starts with taking an honest, hard look at what makes Philadelphia tick, which may include the issues and problems citizens wrestle with every day. There's a lot of active listening, questioning, and discussion among groups of people who may have seen one another as strangers up until that point. The objective is to make sure everyone is heard, even the voices that have traditionally been silent or silenced.

These new connections build commonality and eventually inspiration. That journey generates stories worth sharing, and at that point Mural Arts acts as a facilitator to bring together artists, residents, non-profit leaders, funders, policy-makers, and anyone else needed to express the newfound narrative and mutual respect on an urban wall.

The organization has three core programs that offer unique opportunities for youth searching for their voice through art, people healing from mental health issues or trauma, and people/communities who are restorative-justice participants. These are often the circumstances that isolate people and divide communities, but through Mural Arts Philadelphia they become the stories that unite a city. The murals create understanding because they're in the hands of people who have something they need to say. There's really only one word to describe that: *joy*. §

CHAPTER FIVE

Cities that Offer Joy Win

The main takeaway thus far from this book is cities that offer joy win, which is a very odd premise to hang our hats on. So let's start things off here by giving this concept some structure.

At some point in the past 50 years, urban planners started rethinking how cities should interact with citizens. Industrial factory work was no longer the norm, and the idea of separating where people lived from the smelly places they worked was becoming outdated. It was suggested that cities should offer the ability to live, work, and play.

The concept of LIVE, WORK, PLAY became the bible in municipal-planning circles and mayoral offices. It offered some progress in terms of shortening the distances in our day and creating other efficiencies, but because traditional definitions were used for the words, further change was limited. Most people interpreted LIVE, WORK, PLAY as follows:

- In a city, you LIVE, meaning you have shelter. A bed and pillow and a backyard like everyone else on your street.
- In a city, you WORK, earning a living that allows you to live. For many of us, work gives us our identities and shapes where and what kind of shelters we choose. Live and work are clearly connected. One supports the quality of the other.
- In a city, you PLAY, sort of ... in some way. No one is quite clear how to define PLAY. Maybe it's shopping, going to a restaurant or a movie, though we now shop online, order in, and watch Netflix. Maybe PLAY

OPEN
Live

Work
Play.

is what we do in a park that's usually built on land that can't be used for much else. One thing is certain: PLAY isn't meaningfully connected to LIVE and WORK and it's definitely an afterthought. PLAY is in the category of "nice to have."

Sometimes society can be very literal, which in this case inadvertently led cities to prioritize investments and resources in a LIVE, WORK, PLAY order. The consequences of focusing so heavily on LIVE and WORK meant there were few funds left for PLAY. The distribution of policy-making time, infrastructure resources, city investments, and the desire of cities seemed to be: LIVE 50 percent, WORK 40 percent, PLAY 10 percent.

Using this practical mindset, cities are currently built like machines for the delivery of everyday needs. Citizens play the role of labourer of the machine and consumer of the product. It's more efficient than previously but rather robotic.

Here's our point: if you have a choice in where you live, you'll probably not pick what we just described. Cities should be machines that deliver *joy*. And we should build them following a different order:

- **PLAY:** When you play, you feel joy. You're connected to your surroundings and people. Your body and mind are working the way they were meant to.
- **LIVE:** When people are around places that have the infrastructure for play, they're engaged, growing, and truly living. They have energy and do amazing things. They take pride in what they create and where they live. To be clear, we aren't suggesting areas of play need to be directly connected to people's homes. Play happens beyond backyards, which expands the meaning of LIVE to become something more than entertaining people on our deck.
- **WORK:** The talent most businesses need tends to gravitate to vibrant environments, and in the future that talent will have more freedom to relocate based on personal desires. *The businesses that continue to invest in office and industrial space will want to set up shop where this type of talent and energy already exists.*

> **When people PLAY, they feel JOY and are connected to their surroundings and neighbours.**

The above isn't really an outlandish idea. Innovation is often nothing more than reshuffling the deck based on basic observations of what works in today's world rather than the past. A redistribution of policy-making and city-building energy and investments in the following way will get us closer to cities that are truly sustainable in the 21st century: PLAY 35 percent, LIVE 35 percent, WORK 30 percent.

> **PLAY gives people energy to do amazing things. They take pride in what they create and where they LIVE.**

Today, cities lure businesses and investments through tax breaks that citizens ultimately pay for. Wouldn't it be better if we changed the lure to a talented, energetic, healthy, and stable workforce? When businesses are attracted by a stable pool of talent devoted to the community they live in, businesses will also be more likely to value that whole package and become devoted to the community, as well. As we consider how to shape our cities for the future, perhaps we should ask, How does our city play? How do we want it to play?

Think of this as the new formula for city building: PLAY + LIVE + WORK = JOY.

This is a new path with a very new type of destination for most mid-sized cities. Getting it right will require experimentation and collaboration. Since we believed in the model so much and saw such a big need for change in our community, we started the Joy Experiments as our first steps down this new path.

Scott: My own movement toward the PLAY + LIVE + WORK = JOY model started in Cambridge, Ontario. I was born and raised in the Preston part of Cambridge, and HIP Developments views this city as part of its primary market and corporate home along with Kitchener, Waterloo, and the rest of Waterloo Region. So, because it's where my roots are and where I operate as a real estate developer, I've paid very close attention to the evolution of this city. In this book, Waterloo Region is the backdrop for our Joy Experiments. It's not a big city nor is it small. It was once an industrial centre, but like many mid-sized cities, it's now positioning itself to be a vital part of innovation economy. So this contextual backdrop should provide some legitimacy to the purpose and outcomes of our Joy Experiments.

Several years ago, I was reading a book called *Happy City* by Charles Montgomery, a wonderful study about how urban design shapes our thoughts and behaviour. On weekends, I read a chapter or two and then peered over the top of my book at Cambridge, thinking, *Hmm, I don't think this is a very happy city.* I didn't believe that because I hated the city; I actually care very deeply about it.

Few landmarks represent Cambridge's unhappiness as much as Hespeler Road, a 4.6-kilometre, six-lane street jammed with every possible national retail chain store and fast-food outlet. On either side of the road are parking lots that stretch city block after city block with huge signs. There are sidewalks, but no one ever walks anywhere on Hespeler Road. The only objective of the urban planning was to create space for cars, signs, and strip mall stores.

The intent of anyone coming to this part of town is to drive to the biggest sign you can find, buy something, drive back home, and finally sit in the backyard, family room, or basement. Why was this experience created? Because it was viewed as a practical way to shop. It's not pretty. It's not fun. It's certainly nowhere close to instilling happiness or joy, but it efficiently and robotically gets people from their yards to a store and back again: LIVE + WORK + PLAY = EFFICIENTLY GOOD ENOUGH.

Hespeler Road is "good enough," but the problem with "good enough" is it always gets worse. I carried around my dog-eared copy of *Happy City* and wondered what could be done to change my hometown. HIP was gaining a reputation for building exciting urban condominium projects. We were becoming influential in the community, and I felt that influence was very closely connected to responsibility. What could HIP do to change the continued slow march toward *good enough*?

Around that time, I met John Wright, who owned the Southworks properties along the Grand River in downtown Galt. Southworks was a series of 100-plus-year-old foundries and mills that had been the engine of Galt's past prosperity. John had a reputation for trying to improve Cambridge through unconventional means, so it wasn't surprising that we saw eye to eye on a few things. His property was prime for becoming something more than its most recent incarnation, which was an outlet mall, but the scale of it just didn't align with the terms of his business. After a few inspiring conversations, HIP became owners of the property, and it was now our turn to see if this old engine of a past economy could become the engine of change for Cambridge today.

The first thing I did was toss out the dusty lens of practicality that most people had been looking through for so long. Then I started to make a list of what downtown Galt needed if it was ever going to be a place that attracted investment and population growth. Some of the things that appeared on that list included:

- Celebration
- Play
- Entertainment
- Food, drink, and space to laugh
- Employment opportunities connected to a whole new world of research and knowledge
- Art studios available for free to artists so they can share ideas and create with freedom
- Places to live that are close to it all

The point of my list was to formulate ideas around PLAY + LIVE + WORK = JOY, and I titled the list "Let's Get Happy."

I shared my thoughts with a growing network of people who could wrap their minds around big ideas. They included Rick Haldenby from the University of Waterloo School of Architecture as well as local architects Andrew Bousfield, Patrick Simmons, and Roger Farwell. Roger introduced

Vibrant walls.

Good enough and status quo are barriers to leveraging a city's potential.

me to Paul Kalbfleisch, who has a way of delving into the abstract spaces of big ideas and giving them shape through words, images, and art. He moves fuzzy stuff into the world of action and quickly became my vision partner. Downtown Galt has the Grand River flowing through it and wonderful old architecture, including churches, yet with all that potential it was slowly going nowhere. Surely, with a bit of creative thinking, there was a better future for this part of Ontario.

Over time, the idea of the Gaslight District took shape. It included a public square, event hall, office space, research centre, studios, restaurants, bars, and two towers of condominiums built for real people to live in rather than just being an income source for investors.

In the fall of 2017, we unveiled the Gaslight District, not with a traditional marketing campaign but with a $500,000 party complete with food, drink, two stages, more than 20 musical acts, a market, kids' performances, and an air show that included three fighter jets that caused people to call the police because they thought Cambridge was being invaded!

Intentionally, we went overboard, hoping to give our quiet community a shock of joy. We set a date, with no rain backup, crossed our fingers, and invited the whole city to the *free* event. The weather was beyond perfect. Fifteen thousand people, out of a population of 100,000, attended and had a great time. Cambridge, it turned out, could celebrate and experience joy! People loved the vision of a European-style public square with open-air restaurants, live music, and public art. The condos sold out in a few days. Paul captured the whole moment and energy perfectly in a phrase that would go on to symbolize the project in future marketing: *this is Cambridge as we always dreamed it could be.*

As I stood in the midst of that big, happy day, I realized something everyone had underestimated or lost sight of: there was a lot more positivity in this community than we thought. All it required was leadership.

The appetite for joy demonstrated at the Gaslight District event was enough to make the City of Cambridge and Mayor Doug Craig, an early believer and supporter of joy, pay attention. For the first time in years, city decision-makers could see and feel the civic power of joy in their community. It was easier to imagine that this city contained the energy and desire to do amazing things. The population could demonstrate that they took pride in what they created and where they lived. And if this became more of an everyday occurrence, it wasn't hard to imagine businesses wanting to tap into this type of creativity and energy.

There was still a great deal of work to be done, but a small bridge had been built between the public and private sectors, and the seeds of PLAY + LIVE + WORK = JOY had been planted.

Good Enough Versus Joy

PERHAPS WE SHOULD PROVIDE CLEAR DEFINITIONS OF *good enough* and *joy* because there are likely a few readers pointing fingers and saying, "Can't there be joy in being content with what you have? Isn't it harmful to always want more and better things?" Our answer to the first question is "Yes," while the answer to the second is "Sometimes."

We really don't want to define these words in terms of an attitude toward desire and acquisition because *good enough* and *joy* are two very different things. *Good enough* is a perspective, a defining and concluding point of view: *Things are fine the way they are and for whatever reason they don't need to be better and there's no need to debate or change. Joy*, on the other hand, is an outcome of personal growth and purpose through being connected to something. One is a finite way of thinking; the other is an infinite feeling from activity that provides fulfillment. What we have witnessed is that if you get a group of people thinking in *good enough* terms, there's little room for growth and therefore little room for *joy*.

Here's what this all means for cities. The cities worth exploring and living in offer space for socializing and play, which usually involves a lot of learning and laughter. Your favourite park or market never stops providing *joy*. It always delivers. Cities can be sources of *infinite joy* if the *good enough* perspective is pushed aside.

Joyful spaces don't always have to cost big money, but they do have to possess a big impact that comes from public engagement. Many cities, to be safe and practical, clear a space, plant shrubs, and install benches or paint a mural or two in a back alley. Some may say that's *good enough* or better than nothing. But because they weren't designed to engage the public emotionally, they most likely have zero impact on the community. §

CHAPTER SIX

The Elevator Pitch of a City

Imagine meeting someone for the first time who asks, "Where do you live? What's it like there?" These are seemingly simple questions to answer. This is the elevator pitch of a city, and it's a very important moment in city building because a city is the shared sum of what its citizens think it is. How people answer these questions helps determine how people behave in their cities, and that's a dominant factor in what a city can become — any size of city.

We could call this elevator pitch analogy an issue about brand. Major cities, such as London, England, and New York City, have brands. People from those cities answer questions in consistent ways, and there's almost a city psyche that guides behaviour and decision-making about their futures. But with mid-sized cities, using the word *brand* can confuse the issue because frankly so many mid-sized cities do a poor job of branding. If you scan city or chamber of commerce websites, you'll likely see videos that offer a checklist of amenities that suggest "we have cool things here, too": microbreweries, parks, bike lanes, up-to-date public transit, hipster coffee shops, trendy dining, business start-ups, et cetera. Rather than promoting their uniqueness, which is the foundation of branding, many cities promote their sameness, the opposite of what brands do.

The reason for that likely has to do with the fact that determining and fostering uniqueness in a city is hard work. It's fairly easy to offer a narrative that says we have what everyone else has rather than doing the challenging work of digging deep into a community's culture to understand what uniquely binds and guides citizens in good and bad times.

So are we.
We're cool.

Best coffee shops!
Ours are better.
We're cooler!

[A real identity or brand focuses on what makes a city unique. It's not an exercise in "me, too."]

Paul: Matthew McConaughey, the American actor, is an eloquent city-building supporter of Austin, Texas. I found his articulation of some of the themes to be insightful and poetic. To paraphrase him, while Austin is busy building up and out, it also needs to build deep, focusing on its cultural DNA because that's the deep growth that makes all other kinds of growth sustainable.

Or, to summarize it another way, I could borrow and alter a thought from author and speaker Simon Sinek: it's not what a city has and does that matters; it's *why* it has and does those things that holds its uniqueness and provides an indicator of what the city will become. And a city's *why* is always found in its culture.

I agree with these concepts. True city building starts with cultural DNA and the goal of growing deep.

Many cities have the tendency to commoditize themselves. Every municipality feels the same. Sure, it may be easier to move to a community that already seems familiar, but it's also easy to leave for the next place that also appears familiar and might have better jobs or lower housing costs. *New Yorker* magazine published a somewhat humorous article on this topic entitled "The Unbearable Sameness of Cities." The article's author, Oriana Schwindt, set out to compare cities nearest to the geographic centre of every U.S. state. She makes the same checklist observations you can do by watching city videos:

> It wasn't just the coffee shops — bars, restaurants, even the architecture of all the new housing going up in these cities looked and felt eerily familiar. Every time I walked into one of these places, my body would give an involuntary shudder. I would read over my notes for a city I'd visited months prior and find that several of my observations could apply easily to the one I was currently in.

Basing a community's reputation exclusively on a checklist of amenities does more damage than just the commoditization of mid-sized cities. It ignores the most important reason businesses and people choose where to live — predictability of future success. All cities face change and challenges. It's their cultural roots and identity that hold the predictors of future behaviours.

Years ago, we wondered if New York City would survive 9/11. Of course it did, because

New Yorkers are New Yorkers! The World Trade Center didn't define them. Tenacity did.

In the 1970s, Montreal lost much of its banking industry, along with most of its English-speaking business leadership. It was a struggle, but there was something beneath the skin of that city that allowed people to believe those things didn't define Montreal. It had more to do with being a city where people took their paycheques to bistros on Fridays while people in other Canadian cities brought their weekly pays to the bank. Today, that unique love of life continues to express Montreal's own PLAY, LIVE, WORK experiences such as Quartier des spectacles (QDS), once the red-light district but today the showcase of culture as a key development tool for Montreal. New public spaces and real estate projects have been built that contain engaging world-class digital public art displays. This type of art is the highlight of the area and makes QDS a place best experienced after dark as more than 30 public spaces and sites light up in highly creative ways. The exterior walls of the Grande Bibliothèque and the University of Quebec in Montreal's Pavillon Président-Kennedy are wonderful examples of this lively architectural digital projection technique, often featuring the talents of local creative studios.

Not surprisingly, Montreal has become a global leader in digital animation and entertainment. It's an example of a city's uniqueness and identity remaining consistent through change and actually guiding the community through turbulent times. Montreal's identity isn't a result of the amenities it has; it's the reason it has them and why it will continue to be a centre for vibrant living.

The Joy of Responsibility

THE CITY OF AMERSFOORT IN THE NETHERLANDS IS A MID-SIZED city where people live well and have a decent income and good education. It's nice. But in all this niceness there was a problem — too much municipal bureaucracy designed to ensure things were kept clean, efficient, and *nice*. All the administrative processes were slowing the city down in a world that was speeding up. So, in 2014, the Year of Change was launched, a complete overhaul of the city's administrative processes and activities. It was a shift away from the "command-and-control" role of city hall to facilitating a citizen- or user-driven approach. Shockingly, it was described as an attempt at "letting go."

Well, doesn't that all sound too good to be true? No more fighting city hall. Citizens finally get to do whatever they want and get whatever they desire. Some readers are probably saying "Hallelujah!" while others are crying "Heaven forbid!" However, the reality, as so often is the case, lies in between. The real intent of the Year of Change was to transform the way things got done in Amersfoort into a process of shared responsibility and collective leadership — a collaborative city.

Despite all the difficulties in collaboration, we love the word and intent. That's one of the reasons we cheer on Amersfoort. The other reason is because the city embraces experimentation as the path to a better way of doing things.

One such experiment involved citizen-led urban development. One of the city's old hospitals was marked for demolition, and city council had decided to redevelop the site to become a green space. Residents were already organizing and discussing the pros and cons of a park and what the design should be. Rather than let this turn into argumentative town halls and protests, the administration decided to give the project to the citizens to work out. A citizen park project group was created and handed an "official assignment," including a budget and timelines. The group's task was to organize itself and develop a park plan that included how it would maintain the park over the next 10 years.

The citizen group worked hard — 1,400 hours were put into the effort. The city administration was there to help with guidance and connections, and in the end, the experiment worked. The teams delivered a complete project plan and a unified community ready to endorse, embrace, and care about their new amenity.

This experiment and others like it led to the full launch of the Year of Change as the city leadership began to realize that what was once inconceivable was actually a sustainable new way of city building. Amersfoort held a conference on this new collaboration approach that was well attended by citizens, elected officials, and civil servants. People discussed what they wanted from their city and eventually created 10 city projects out of more than 100 ideas. §

Paul: I visited Montreal's Quartier des spectacles while doing research on world-class methods of activating public space. The technology and techniques are quite impressive, but what struck me most of all was how those tricks were used to metaphorically project the city's culture back to its citizens. There was never a generic moment that said, "We have cool things, too." I felt that the area instinctively reminded everyone about who they were. The content, style of public art, and events made Montrealers feel more like Montrealers.

The whole experience greatly influenced my "Creative Intersections" public space strategy. After a few visits, I was inspired to see if identifying and celebrating city culture could also be achieved in smaller mid-sized cities. This type of "identity" work is the much-needed ingredient in mid-sized city branding. Forget about a logo, slogan, and list of cool "me, too" things. None of that answers the question "What will your city become?"

The stories we tell about our hometowns matter a lot. They can result in a community confidence that propels a city forward. When the identity is shared broadly, it has a way of pulling people together as they strive to overcome challenges. The other thing it creates is a sense of community lineage that connects the stories of a city's past trials, successes, and behaviours and highlights how they manifest themselves in present-day situations. It places a responsibility upon current citizens to pass the torch to the next generation. Lineage implies that everyone has a role and responsibility for what their city is and will become. It doesn't matter if the community in question is Stratford, Ontario, or New York City — collective identity and community lineage are the heartbeats that will keep mid-sized cities alive and even potentially become wildly successful in our changing times.

Hamilton, Ontario, offers a great example of identity being employed to wrestle with the issues of future growth. The "other" city on Lake Ontario, as it used to be called by Torontonians, is going through a renaissance and resurgence all at once. Since it's situated so close to Toronto, and artists were the first to see the value of low rents and old factories, it has a new nickname — "The Brooklyn of Toronto." But rather than just fully embrace this "we're cool, too" moniker and all that goes with it, the community is using its identity and roots to help it decide what it should become.

Becoming a suburb of Toronto or a distinct thriving city offering people a community where they can PLAY, LIVE, WORK are the two potential paths Hamilton faces. The true nickname of the city is "The Hammer," which carries attributes of its "Steeltown" past and a rough-and-tumble personality expressed through stories of adversity and teamwork. That identity, rooted in its factory-union history, is part of the debate. Will Hamilton be a place where importance is placed on collective approaches to growth that reflect the traditions of its labour-influenced past, or will it become another example of gentrification? We don't know and we aren't taking sides. The important thing is that Hamilton understands what it is and is using that knowledge to guide its future. It's already becoming a rough-and-tumble, colourful artistic centre with a lively James Street North social scene, film stages, and studios being created in old warehouses. We do hope that somehow there will be a form of unique Hamilton Joy on Lake Ontario.

Scott: I was thinking a lot about Waterloo Region's identity or brand. To simplify my thoughts, I asked myself: "What's Waterloo Region's elevator pitch?" I know most people jump to phrases like *tech community* or *innovation hub*, but in my heart I knew that only represented part of who we are and could sense backlash against that identity taking over our community. Most citizens don't work in that sector and resent how insular that group can sometimes be. No one likes to talk about it, but it's true.

Our other approach seemed to be to throw out a bunch of different identities in the hope something would stick. At any given time, we're:

- The Toronto–Waterloo tech corridor
- Maple Valley
- Quantum Valley
- The Mennonite region with barn-raising imagery
- Oktoberfest
- One of Canada's fastest-growing cities
- A place with a small-town feel and relatively affordable housing

I couldn't say any of these were wrong, but I knew none of them tapped into a collective community energy that could build a vibrant and joyful place to PLAY, LIVE, WORK and define a unique joy.

The one attempt at branding that I disliked the most was "Silicon Valley of the North." A successful brand has never been built by openly borrowing its uniqueness. Worse still, comparing Waterloo Region to Silicon Valley is selling my hometown short. We act upon a belief in community collaboration, and Silicon Valley's behaviour is the very antithesis of that. It believes in harsh competition and the overhyped glory of "last man standing." Maybe our collaborative approach has its roots in Mennonite folklore or in a community of immigrants trying to build better lives. I honestly don't know, but what I do understand is that it stuck so well that we tend to take it for granted. I've always been impressed by how the business community in Waterloo Region will help or provide a connection if you need it to assist you in moving forward.

I began to wonder: Can an identity be built, or was it one of those "if you got it you got it, and if you don't you don't" situations? Toronto suggests that it can, in fact, be created if you know something about your past and can tap into the opportunities that change brings.

In the 1950s, Toronto was very white, Anglo-Saxon, and conservative. Torontonians' image of their city was a place of business where you grew up with the Union Jack, went to work, ate apple pie at Fran's, and watched the Toronto Maple Leafs. "Toronto the Good" was perhaps a little boring. If you wanted fun, you went to Buffalo where things were exciting. The situation might never have changed if it wasn't for the tragic exodus, due to the Front de libération du Québec (FLQ) crisis, of English-speaking people in Montreal in the 1970s that brought a group of wealthy business leaders and most of the Canadian banks to Toronto.

> **Ultimately, an identity should predict, or at least influence, what a city will become.**

Toronto also benefited from a wave of entrepreneurial immigrants from all over the world. This built upon the historic neighbourhood design of the city that once put the Irish in one area, the Anglicans in another, and the Italians across town. But now neighbourhoods became a tool to celebrate differences rather than segregate them. With these changes, Toronto began to think of itself as an international city of neighbourhoods. That internal perception changed how people interacted with the city and one another. It became one of the best places to watch soccer's World Cup. When Italy played Portugal, or any other country, those neighbourhoods buzzed with excitement. Toronto is now a vibrant global community. The restaurant scene also improved greatly, but unfortunately the Leafs haven't ... well, there's always hope.

This shows that identities can be formed and adapted. With that belief in hand, we decided to learn about Austin, Texas.

Austin is one of the coolest cities in the United States and is the home of South by Southwest, the film, interactive media, and music festival. However, it wasn't always the hipster/tech centre it is today. As recently as 30 years ago, it was a struggling university town. There were very few jobs for graduating students, so most left. The mortgage and real estate crisis of the 1990s also hit the city very hard. Downtown Austin, which is full of buzz today, was a dark and dangerous place. To reverse fortunes, city leadership tackled many issues and advanced several strategies, but a key turning point came as they addressed the issue of city identity.

We spoke with Cookie Ruiz, one of many city leaders involved in turning things around and executive director of Ballet Austin. She recalled a moment when conversations were full of envy for cities like Nashville, which called itself the "Country Music Capital," or Seattle with its "City of Music" moniker. One community leader boldly stated that Austin should make the claim to be the "Live Music Capital of the World." The city certainly had a history as a music centre due to the successful TV show *Austin City Limits* and as the town that gave Janis Joplin, Jim Morrison, and Stevie Ray Vaughan their early breaks. But to claim "Live Music Capital of the World" was, as Cookie put it, wildly *audacious* ... so much so that it made people stop in their tracks and pay attention. They had to admit if felt good to say it and fun to believe it. Soon, with audacious determination, city leaders got to work making sure they could live up to the claim. With an aspirational identity that reflected the essence of the decade-old unofficial city slogan "Keep Austin Weird," they had a new focus as they fixed up parks and changed city bylaws to make it easier for bands to unload their equipment in front of the many downtown bars.

Identity should be authentic and something everyone can embrace, not just one sector of the community.

This identity shift helped change things for Austin. Downtown was alive with an atmosphere that blended perfectly with the university crowd. Dell, the computer company, and other tech firms moved to Austin because they wanted to tap into that university talent. With its audacious identity, it made sense to take a chance on a music festival they called South by Southwest. Austin still has its issues, one of which is rising housing costs due to all its success, but it offers citizens a uniquely Austin PLAY, LIVE, WORK formula. Clearly, Austin was an inspiration, and with the word *audacious* ringing in our ears, that got us thinking.

Paul: I'm sure someone once said, "If you want to know where you're going, take a good look at where you came from," or something to that effect. We saw how Austin, as audacious as it is, still tried to be true to elements of its past. So we looked back, as well.

Scott knew that our region had a rich history of industry and invention from the 1890s to the 1960s. Kitchener was once referred to as the industrial heartbeat of Canada. Lang Tanning Co. was the largest tannery in the British Empire. This was the community that gave the world Kaufman's Sorel footwear, Crown Royal rye whisky, Hush Puppies, and, one day, BlackBerry.

I told Scott it also gave the world Bauer Supreme hockey skates. As a teenager, I worked summers in the Bauer factory, and all the hockey greats of that time came to Kitchener to have their skate boots custom-fitted by the ladies in the sewing room. Even the Russians wore Bauer. Today, Bauer, now owned by Peak Achievement Athletics, is still a dominant brand in hockey.

As a businessman, Scott knew that major successes like Crown Royal and Hush Puppies don't just happen. They're the result of creative problem-solving minds. Being the bold and sometimes audacious thinker he is, Scott proposed that if Austin can be the Live Music Capital of the World, why can't we be the Creative Capital of Canada?

A city's identity isn't something a committee creates or is authorized by a city council. It's a collaborative effort by private, public, social, and business sectors. Before we started our Joy Experiment in identity, there had been many public-sector-led initiatives to define Waterloo Region's "brand," but most of them struggled to land on something that had broad acceptance. In fact, when we began canvassing community leaders to participate in our efforts, many said they'd been through so many of these discussions that they weren't interested. This type of reaction only increased our belief that it was time for the private sector to take a turn providing the leadership needed to create a unifying identity. And so we set out to define what the Creative Capital of Canada meant and design a network of supporters.

We know, we know, most of you are still stuck a few paragraphs back on the word *creative*. You might assume the word means art, music, writing ... or dressing funny, and have no idea what it has to do with an industrial heritage, hockey skates, or uniting Waterloo Region. We hear you saying, "Surely, Montreal is the Creative Capital of Canada." Or maybe Vancouver is. Let's clarify what creativity is. It's a process or way of thinking, and that kind of thought can be applied to any topic, not just art, music, writing, et cetera. It's the ability to solve problems and make new things happen through the use of fresh perspectives. And here's the big news: everyone is creative. Kevin Ashton, in his book *How to Fly a Horse*, sums it up best:

> Everyone can create, and we can show that fairly conclusively. The challenging part is that there is no magic moment to creation. Creators spend almost all their time creating, persevering despite doubt, failure, ridicule, and rejection until they succeed in making something new and useful. There are no tricks, shortcuts, or get-creative-quick schemes. The process is ordinary, even if the outcome is not.

When people hear this definition, most feel it describes something they've experienced at work, home, or in relationship to their hobbies. It's true — we all create things that are new and useful.

Being creative is like being able to throw a baseball. We can all do it, but some of us are better at it than others. The biggest difference between most of us and people who are good at being creative, innovative, or solving problems is the fear of failure. Failing is part of the creative process, and too many of us were raised to think failing is bad. But ask inventors and they'll tell you failing is good. It gets you closer to the right way of doing things. To quote Thomas Edison, "I have not failed. I've just found 10,000 ways that won't work."

Waterloo Region has had more than its share of fearless Thomas Edisons who turned out to be very creative problem-solvers. A hundred years ago creative minds turned our community into an industrial powerhouse in the British Empire. Another generation of problem-solvers led our transition into the innovation economy. Jacob Kaufman, Louis Breithaupt, Hugh McCulloch, Hartman Krug, Roy Charles Bauer, and Mike Lazaridis drove an inventive spirit that gave birth to all their companies' products. We should also mention firms such as the Tiger Brand Knitting Company, Home Hardware, and the University of Waterloo, as well as 2018 Physics Nobel Prize winner Donna Strickland, to name just a few other successes. And we did all that through hard work. This type of creativity is the thing that tech start-ups, workers in advanced manufacturing, gardeners, artists, educators, all of us, have in common.

The Creative Capital of Canada is the audacious title that can unify the community and set a positive course for the future. And we have the stories. Not long after we began focusing on the region's problem-solving creativity, we found a wealth of historical stories about our creativity and invention. Thanks to Waterloo Region, the world was introduced to these innovations:

- **Blue Box** recycling program, which helped cities divert waste and extend the longevity of landfill sites. Many cities around the world follow this program.
- **Grand River Conservation Authority**, the first watershed management program in Canada, which changed the Grand from a very polluted river into a healthy, beautiful space that's home to bald eagles.
- **Starcross 288 Chicken**, a hen bred to lay 288 eggs per year. That type of chicken became the leader in the production of eggs everywhere.
- **Form-Fitting Underwear** by a company in Galt that made the first such underwear guaranteed not to shrink. The firm promised to replace any that did. Use your imagination to picture what they might have looked or felt like!
- **IMAX**, started by Graeme Ferguson, Roman Kroitor, Robert Kerr, and William C. Shaw, who were high school students at Galt Collegiate Institute when they started thinking about ways to make huge movie screens. They went on to invent IMAX, which lets people watch movies six storeys tall. That's a big idea.
- **Restorative Justice**, in which Mark Yantzi, a fill-in probation officer, used a case in 1974 in Elmira, Ontario, involving youth vandalism to set the framework of restorative justice whereby perpetrators meet victims to apologize and offer restitution. The Elmira Case represented the beginning of a social movement to change the way Canadians deal with crime.
- **Electrohome**, a company that invented a machine (the Circa 75 — a "combination radio-turntable-intercom-television-telephone prototype") that looked like a living-room table and did what the internet does today. It built the machine 30 years before the internet existed.
- **BlackBerry**, the first smartphone. It changed how we communicate. We wouldn't have Instagram without it.
- **Teledyne DALSA**, a technology invented by a company that powers Google Earth and the pictures we see from the Mars Rover.
- **Artificial Cattle Insemination**, developed in 1954 by the Waterloo Cattle Breeders Association, the first organization in the world to use frozen semen to artificially inseminate cattle.
- **Check Engine Light**, invented by Wilfred H. Schlee in 1924, the signal light on a car's instrument panel that warns of low oil pressure.

The above list could go on and on. The Creative Capital of Canada for Waterloo Region felt very right to us. We believed we'd landed on an element of our community culture that had the potential to

- resonate authentically,
- be embraced by everyone in the community, and
- be the genesis of a cultural lineage and a predictor of what the community could become in the future.

The concept was discussed with business leaders, and there was genuine interest. People wanted stories and a fresh way to talk about our community. Our first Joy Experiment was showing signs of life — there was potential. We knew the real objective was to find ways for this identity to uniquely influence our own PLAY, LIVE, WORK = JOY formula. Also, we knew the path started with telling our community's stories.

Scott: We were determined to make the Gaslight District a place where the stories of Cambridge and Waterloo Region were told. As a result, all the public installation art focuses on the stories and importance of the Grand River — our river!

One piece of art, the living architecture sculpture *Meander*, created by the University of Waterloo's School of Architecture faculty member Philip Beesley, uses the shape and flow of the Grand River to express how new solutions can be found in the blending of science, technology, engineering, arts, and math.

Meander is one of the first big cultural storytelling tools of the Creative Capital of Canada. Everyone, especially children, will be able to look up at this beautiful, joyful work and say, "This is us. This is our future."

Love your neighbourhood.

CHAPTER SEVEN

You Attract What You Celebrate

Learning How to Claim Our Identity

This chapter covers one long experiment that for a while didn't progress as well as we'd hoped. But as is so often the case, through that struggle came insight and a better path forward. That's the creative way and an appropriate journey for the Creative Capital of Canada.

Scott: The Creative Capital of Canada, as described in the previous chapter, felt very right to us. We believed that a unifying definition of creativity gave our community the ability to attribute meaning to Waterloo Region's past successes and accomplishments. We also hoped it would give present and future deeds some higher purpose. As we shopped the concept around, many community leaders started to feel the aspirational qualities of the word *creativity* under our definition. At one presentation in Cambridge, a woman thanked me for introducing a new narrative to the community, one that wasn't consumed with negativity; a narrative that could give her children a reason for thinking their home, Waterloo Region, could offer them a future.

Clearly, we had early hints we were on to something, but there was also a sense of "So now what?" How do we turn the Creative Capital of Canada into a movement in the style of Austin, Texas? After all, an identity isn't much good if it isn't claimed by the citizens and helps shape community confidence. In many ways, Waterloo Region typifies the challenges faced by many mid-sized cities. Globalization, urbanization, and the tech revolution were forcing our community to think of economic competition in global terms. While we liked the feeling of a slower, more affordable pace of life, that simply wasn't the

Cultures and cities attract what they celebrate. What they don't celebrate they lose.

reality of our future. Our community was, and still is, in the midst of rapid change. Waterloo Region had a strong need to attract world-class talent as it advanced deeper into the innovation economy. In fact, attracting talent was seen as an economic development bottleneck.

A civic identity can really help in times of change. If it's embraced by everyone, it can provide leaders and citizens with a common purpose. It can be that sticky emotional fabric that bonds people in action and vision. In fact, that might be an even more valuable benefit of identity than the obvious external promotional activities. If truth be told, we weren't all that concerned about logos and the usual tools of branding. We believed the real job was to embed the Creative Capital of Canada message into the minds and hearts of the people who lived in our community as an authentic reflection of our past and future.

We knew we weren't celebrating the creative talent of our past and present as well as other places in the world. Being celebrators was a little counter to the evident German, Mennonite, and Scottish humble heritage of the area.

I'll admit I'm a bit bold and blunt at times. Maybe a lot of the time. But my approach to challenges is to dive in and look for the positive opportunities that might be hidden. We'd developed a way of talking about Waterloo Region's past and present that seemed inclusive and inspiring. We'd uncovered an abundance of stories that could be proudly celebrated. I'm not one to wait around for permission to celebrate. It seemed to me we were at an "Austin moment" — a time for audacity, and I was quite comfortable having HIP lead the way by example.

The Creative Capital of Canada wasn't meant to be a formal organization, committee, or official government-sanctioned council. We weren't telling city or regional officials they had to now adopt a new "brand." It was meant to be a social movement propelled by people who cared and had vision and energy. To lead the way, HIP launched its own voice and perspective on the inclusiveness of creativity.

HIP's perspective was conveyed through a video meant to rally the broad community and embolden people to celebrate their own creative abilities. The video was called *Just Like You* and the narration was as follows:

> Who among us is creative? Is it the person with a paintbrush in the hand? Or is being creative more outgoing than that? Is it the person with a guitar over the shoulder? To be creative, do you

have to write in rhymes … and speak that way … all the time?

Do you have to dance; do you have to sing? Do you have to dress a certain way to be creative? Maybe clothing helps and maybe creative people do these things, but creative people also shape things with their hands … They use their minds to make things grow … *just like you!* Creative people are effective communicators … And they work to understand problems and they make beautiful solutions … *just like you!* They find ways of making zeros and ones add up to big things … and turn big things into small, delicate, beautiful things. Creative people are brave. They put opposites together.

Creative people care. Creative people imagine what hasn't happened yet … *just like you!*

What's creativity? Well, that's when we take a group of people, *just like us*, and combine our abilities, talents, and courage to see what big thing we can make happen next. The Creative Capital of Canada is right here … in *all of us*.

Accompanying the above words were images of everyday people doing everyday things. The message: we all do creative things, we all solve problems. HIP distributed the message to community leaders and bought advertising time at local movie theatres. It was a message of honest belief on the part of HIP Developments, who were interested in building personal creative confidence as well as community confidence. With the release of this video, HIP invited others in the community to express their own points of view. Our journey into celebrating our community's identity had begun.

Paul: While all this work was going on, the Toronto Raptors were marching toward the 2019 National Basketball Association championship. That was impressive, and so was the way in which "We the North" had become a national rally cry. It wasn't just describing a basketball team anymore; it was an emotional national expression of today's version of Canada, no longer staid and polite. The most important word in the line became *We* as Canadians across the country wrapped themselves in the phrase as if it were our flag. Bianca Andreescu, the first Canadian tennis player to win the U.S. Open singles, became #SheTheNorth, and U.S. sportscasters started to refer to our country as "The North."

"We the North" reminded me of something I always knew but had lost sight of: strong cultural identities rely heavily on symbols. The Creative Capital of Canada had the stories but perhaps not a cultural tattoo like "We the North." It may be easy to dismiss symbols and cultural tattoos as things that only belong to sports teams and perhaps global cities — think of "I ♥ New York." But then there are our friends back at the Austin Local Business Alliance with their cultural phrasing "Keep Austin Weird," which wasn't really planned but worked, not because it's funny and cool but because it's the essence of the way people in Austin think, behave, and make decisions.

That way of thinking made Austin a tech centre and led to the decisions that turned South by Southwest into, well, *South by Southwest!* Am I surprised that "Keep [City] Weird" has popped up in Portland, Indianapolis, and other cities? No. Am I surprised it has little impact in those places? No, because it represents nothing authentic about those cities. To know if a symbol or artifact has the power to change a culture is often tricky. In the case of "Keep Austin Weird," does its power exist because it summarizes a culture? But enough about Austin. There are other examples of mid-sized cities engaging their citizens in identity building, such as Edmonton, Alberta.

The Edmonton story may not be our Joy Experiment, but nonetheless it's a good example. And we're cool with that. It's our not-so-secret wish that Joy Experiments become a worldwide movement in city building. The Edmonton story makes us want to visit that city and drink the water.

Edmonton is the most northerly major city in Canada. That makes it cold and dark in the winter. It's known for having the world's largest shopping mall and for being the place where Wayne Gretzky reinvented hockey. We're sure it's known for many other great things, but it just doesn't register in the minds of a lot of Canadians, much less the global perspective. And yet, from what we've learned, people who live there love it.

Like a lot of mid-sized cities Edmonton was constantly feeling it needed to revamp its image and went through a period of using generic phrases that could work almost anywhere. In fact, most of the phrases were being employed in other cities except one: "It's cooler here." While people in Edmonton desired a better identity, they also grew tired of trying. So a group of marketers, journalists, and passionate citizens took it upon themselves to dig deep into what they felt was the essence of Edmonton. Similar to our work in Waterloo Region, they found a recurring story about how good things happen in that city. Edmonton's DNA is that of a frontier city full of risk-takers who reject hierarchy in favour of meaningful collaboration. Everything good in Edmonton, whether it a festival or a tech company, involved those types of risk-taking personalities and their passions, an interesting cultural narrative that helped to drive who they might become in the future. But what's more interesting is how they put, or invited, that identity into the hearts of Edmontonians.

The group created a citizen board to map out how to engage the public in the narrative insight it had discovered. One of the first successful activities was to turn all its research into an online blog full of stories of the Edmonton way of making things happen. It got noticed, and the group boldly launched a community-building activity called "Make Something Edmonton." That might sound like an advertising slogan, but if nothing else, it sounds better than "It's cooler here." However, it was really a call-to-action program asking citizens to go out and make something happen. Anything. Just go, take a risk, collaborate, and make something the Edmonton way.

> **How a culture celebrates its identity is as unique as the identity itself.**

Perhaps "Make Something Edmonton" was just the right type of dare to align with Edmonton's DNA, because it succeeded in authentic engagement. More than 1,500 public-led projects were submitted — everything from decorating bridges to founding new businesses. The stories were collected and posted. The blog and website became a mix of new and historical stories. People were no longer debating identity in conference rooms with consultants. They were making their identity.

This movement also propelled tangible change. When processes and bylaws worked against this risk-taking and collaborative identity, people demanded change and succeeded. Posted on outdoor walls of businesses were sentences such as "Take a risk. It's the most Edmonton thing you can do."

"Make Something Edmonton" is a great example of experimentation, identity celebration, and the power of narratives and artifacts. The core narrative was eventually embraced in a variety of ways by the Edmonton Economic Development Corporation (now the Explore Edmonton Corporation) and city hall. Most importantly, Edmonton created an identity that allowed it to define its own version of PLAY, LIVE, WORK = JOY.

These types of stories that contain forms of populism celebration encouraged us. We should take a moment to state that when we use the term *populism*, we aren't referring to the political definitions filling the news on a daily basis. We're talking about grassroots movements that find a way to simplify meaning in a way that makes it easier to fit into people's hearts and emotions. "We the North" isn't political in the sense of being right or left wing. But it's certainly populism.

Without even knowing about the Edmonton project, we had set up similar activities that included the website creativecapitalofcanada.ca. It's a repository, or library, of all our historical problem-solving stories and new items that feature the efforts of today's generation of creative minds. The community was encouraged through a social media campaign to contribute its own stories and sign up to be public members of the movement. The goal was to not just have a place where the community could learn about its own heritage but for it also to be a place where people from outside the community could witness Waterloo Region's belief in, and celebration of, its identity.

To spread audacious passion for the Creative Capital of Canada, we also felt we needed our own simple, bold cultural tattoo that allowed people to express their individual and collective identity the way "We the North" had. Our cultural tattoo became "Creativity Is Right Here." It carried multiple meanings: creativity is right here in Waterloo Region and creativity is right here in me as an individual. Both sides of that pride could help build a confident and inclusive identity.

Scott: I wanted, and still want, a giant flag on Highway 401 as you enter Waterloo Region that's emblazoned with "Creativity Is Right Here — The Creative Capital of Canada."

"Creativity Is Right Here" stickers, window decals, and pins were produced and distributed through the Business Improvement Areas of Kitchener, Waterloo, and Cambridge, as well as those cities' chambers of commerce. Additional pins were produced that visually represented famous Waterloo Region innovations. There were lapel-sized blue boxes, BlackBerrys, 3D glasses (for IMAX), and the Wil-Tel Automatic Oil Signal lights.

The local Business Improvement Areas (BIAs) also showed their support by participating in the creation and hanging of banners in the downtown cores that carried the "Creativity Is Right Here" phrase along with visual representations of Waterloo Region's creativity.

Scott: HIP's financial investment and commitment of energy made all these infrastructure projects possible. We did it because we believed in the vision and the community. And we knew leadership had to start somewhere.

We'd seen this great TED Talk video about how to start a movement. It showed a guy at an outdoor concert dancing wildly and everyone sitting back watching with no intention of participating. Eventually, one person joined him. Now there were two people making it easier for a few more to join. Once the group got to 10, well, of course, everyone felt the need to be part of it because they didn't want to be left out. I knew I was going to be the one person wildly dancing, but I didn't know I'd have to dance alone for so long. TED Talks are very short, so maybe that created unreal expectations on my part.

Experiments by their very nature don't always go to plan. If they did, they'd hardly be experiments. There was a lot of excitement about the Creative Capital of Canada, and it continued to be positively received. However, the hope that others would be bold enough to join in and take up the challenge to celebrate fell short of the goal. Perhaps the idea of an open social movement was too abstract. Certainly, there was a desire for some structure: specific projects, defined roles, concerns about permissions … and then there was that word we disliked so much — *committee*. From our perspective, there had already been too many identity and branding committees that led nowhere. We didn't want to fall into that trap again.

There are times when a change in perspective transforms the world. We were facing one of those moments. We'd thought that populism tactics were the tools to identity celebration and success. It certainly seemed that way when you looked at Austin and Edmonton. But the more we scrutinized other successes, the more we saw that the real key to success was to engage people in a way that aligned with their values and behaviours. Austin, for all its wonderful success, can be a confusing and misleading example. Populist tactics work in Austin because Texas is a populist and audacious culture. Being the "Live Music Capital" and "Keep Austin Weird" are the kind of bold dares aligned with the city's way of turning ideas into action. In Edmonton, the "Make Something Edmonton" program asked people to do what they do best and believe in — creating things. Again, this was in line with Edmonton's values, and that's why the populist tactics worked. The program resulted in populist activity; it didn't start with it.

Waterloo Region is a community of creative problem-solvers, and we weren't giving them a defined problem to solve. We were asking them to do something a bit uncomfortable for their cultural humbleness. Our narrative was right, and the cultural tattoos were promising. But we weren't engaging people the correct way.

Scott: Around this time, Paul and I were meeting regularly. We discussed what we felt was falling short of expectations and what we'd learned in the experiment thus far. It was during these discussions that the idea of cultural lineage came about.

A cultural lineage suggests that a community's behaviours can be traced to past events, and, more importantly, there's an expectation that the behaviours will be carried into the future. In this narrative, it's the responsibility of the current generation to keep cultural behaviours alive for the next generation. That seemed like a challenge our community of problem-solvers could respond to.

Over the years, our community had focused much of its energy on attracting creative talent from other parts of the world to our educational institutions such as the University of Waterloo, with its highly rated engineering, science, and computer studies programs. However, the community didn't have a corresponding program that made our kids aspire to be part of today's action. If we could find a way to involve community leaders in that issue, we could celebrate our past and present identity through building supportive infrastructure for the next generation. We thought of it as passing the "creative baton."

I'm passionate about our community's youth. I still walk the streets I was raised on, and now my own kids join me on those walks. Naturally, I want them to have all the opportunities to succeed that I did. And I want them to have the option of succeeding without leaving home. I think it's important that all kids feel that Waterloo Region has room for their successes. A better distribution of the region's future success starts with a better distribution of the fundamentals of creativity.

Here Comes the Clusterwohnung

OWNING, OR SIMPLY BEING ABLE TO RENT, SOME FORM OF SHELTER has been viewed as rather fundamental to mid-sized city living for quite a while — at least since the 1950s. However, that concept is starting to become a lofty and hard-to-reach benchmark for many communities. In Waterloo Region, trying to solve affordable-housing issues used to be the domain of church groups trying to find ways to help the obviously less fortunate. But now it's become a problem for even people with average-paying jobs. And when the community's ability to offer affordable home ownership becomes a talent recruitment issue for the local innovation economy, well, then we have a problem that everyone's paying attention to.

Solving housing issues such as these puts pressure on everyone, from politicians to social service organizations and even real estate developers. This is partly due to the fact that while everything about these problems is rapidly changing, including the makeup of the family unit, our perceptions of a "home" haven't changed much at all. Yes, we want the affordability issues corrected, but we don't really want to give up much. More affordable-housing units sounds like a good idea as long as it's in a neighbourhood across town, and while we want to make affordable home ownership an easier goal to achieve, is society willing to give up the idea of a backyard, garage, and his or her bathrooms?

In the condominium development sector, we've been primarily focused on one-bedroom-plus-den units as an investment vehicle, and to a lesser degree, two bedrooms for the older downsizer market. I think we are slow at realizing that a condo is quickly becoming the new starter home, and we haven't mastered how to design for that need. Part of the process for solving the affordable housing/ownership puzzle is to let go of past housing expectations and entertain the idea there might be different ways to divide and share the spaces we live in. To help shift our perspectives, let us introduce you to the *Clusterwohnung*, a German word for "cluster apartment." To many of us, it might be a very radical shift in living, but our point is to entertain the idea for a moment and see what we can learn from this funny-sounding Joy Experiment.

Clusterwohnungs are a form of hybrid apartment living. They're small private apartments combined with shared residence spaces. The idea is growing in popularity in Germany, Switzerland, and other European countries. What they offer residents is a very large living area with communal kitchens, living rooms, and dining spaces. These areas are then combined or connected to smaller private units that offer individuals their own bedroom, bathroom, kitchenettes, et cetera. In anyone's home, there are spaces that don't get used as often as others. The *Clusterwohnung* concept maximizes the usage of those areas by making them, and their costs, shared. In an age where many people feel isolated and suffer from depression, having a home with a built-in community is an interesting idea.

If you're lucky enough to have spent most of your life in single-family houses, *Clusterwohnung* may seem like an inconceivable lifestyle. But the future is going to look very different from the past. It always does. Entertaining the unconceivable opens the door to the possible. And we need more possible. §

Confidence grows by learning that even failure, and the insights gained from it, is a path to eventual success.

The most important outcome of the creative lineage planning was the idea of the Youth Creativity Fund. It was born out of the reality that creative skills will continue to grow in demand in our quickly changing world. Knowledge alone isn't a critical differentiator in people's careers, thanks to Google. And today, algorithms rather than people process data and predicts trends. But problem-solving creativity remains the only source of new perspectives, ideas, and invention.

The Youth Creativity Fund is a tool to extend our creative lineage by connecting creative projects designed by students and teachers with needed financial resources supplied by people wanting to see our youth build their creative muscle and confidence. That creative confidence can only be developed through students having the opportunity to try, experiment, fail, and eventually succeed.

The fund is structured so that students in Grades 4 through 12 and teachers can apply online to get financial assistance for creativity-oriented programs, exercises, or projects they're interested in pursuing. The funding grants range between $500 and $2,500.

The Youth Creativity Fund isn't intended to reward "winners" or force students to achieve tactical milestones. Instead, the fund is designed to build the creative confidence of our youth by supporting their exploration of a new idea, including the taking of risks, and accepting and learning from failure. Creative confidence isn't the blind belief that every project will succeed. Confidence grows by learning that even failure, and the insights gained from it, is a path to eventual success.

When we brought the idea of the Youth Creativity Fund and creative lineage to community leaders, the reaction was immediate and positive. This was something they were willing to support financially, and they understood and accepted their role in making sure the region's creative baton was being passed on to the next generation. Other programs and mentoring possibilities started to take shape with the help of the Waterloo Region Business and Education Partnership (BEP), our fund co-sponsor. This group is a charity created by local education and business leaders with a common belief that when youth have access to the information, skills, and connections they need to be successful in their future careers, they'll inevitably make our workforce, economy, and community much stronger. As a result of this belief, BEP works with secondary school students to help them better understand and prepare for the world of work by fashioning learning opportunities with local employers and industry professionals.

Resilience.

Our community has a track record of understanding the value of education and supporting it. The University of Waterloo, known throughout the world as a top-tier school for science, engineering, and computer technology, was created with the guiding values of a strong connection between academia, industry, government, and business. Its inception was also supported by local members of all those sectors, resulting in the first co-op education programs in Canada. The Youth Creativity Fund partnership with BEP replicated the spirit of that style of collaboration, but unlike the global mandate of the university, the focus of the fund was on younger local students.

This was a big moment for us. We had engagement with the people who could make a difference, and we had tangible plans to ensure the next generation of creative minds in Waterloo Region was going to be supported. Perhaps it wasn't the Austin, Texas, moment we set out to create, but it was the beginning of a movement true to the culture of Waterloo Region. Learning the importance of finding an authentic way to engage the public in the celebration and embracing of community identity was a significant lesson for us.

In the future, we'll return to the populist tactics we developed once we gain greater traction with the Youth Creativity Fund and other youth-oriented projects. We still want to bring the "Creativity Is Right Here" rally cry to life. We still want to see the flags and T-shirts. It will come.

Infrastructure for the human spirit.

CHAPTER EIGHT

The Yardstick Is Youth

Walt Disney once said, "Our greatest natural resource is the minds of our children." So true. This chapter involves a lot of back-and-forth dialogue because it reflects our debates and very personal passions regarding today's youth and the role they play in city building — an ever-expanding focus of our Joy Experiments.

Much of society's outlook on life and the choices we make are based on our assumptions about the future. This goes well beyond waking up cheery and full of optimism one morning because the afternoon's plan includes meeting a friend and going to a movie or baseball game. This attitude runs the stock market, elections, and where we choose to live. When we feel good about what the future holds, we invest money, time, and passion in it. If we don't think the future holds promise, some of us set out to change the circumstances for the better, while others simply trade in the circumstances for a new set of options; they sell off stock, move somewhere else, or simply disengage from the world around them. Today, as things feel really difficult everywhere, society, and especially our youth, are evolving into a culture of negation. In an effort to deal with all the anxiety and overstimulation around us, people use numbness as a coping skill and erect barriers of nothingness through the overuse of beige interior design, endless hours of binge-watching Netflix, and ordering home-delivered meals. Fatigued by uncertainty and change, people just want to be left alone. The level of energy this drains from small and mid-sized communities is frightening.

Paul: I once went to an art gallery showing the work of a photographer whose subject matter was small rural towns. Each photo was the straight line of buildings on a main street. The photographs were beautiful, with big blue prairie skies filling most of the images. But they were also mainly ghost towns or towns on death's door, which created an uneasy mood. In the architectural details of the old buildings could be seen hope and optimism. Once, people were full of belief for their community and put a lot of sweat into making it a lovely place. The populations grew, and in the photos were additions that had been put on buildings or architectural styles that had changed on the outer limits of the community. But clearly something had happened. The population growth turned into decline, and as more people left, other people wanted to leave.

That's a lot to read into a photograph, but it seemed so obvious. The viewer couldn't help but want to know how the once unthinkable could happen in a way that nothing could stop the exodus when it started.

You don't need to go to an art gallery to see this sort of thing. We all drive through those small towns that don't seem to have a point anymore because some new technical advancement like the railway passed them by. When we see older people in the towns, we don't really think twice. Of course there are old people there. This place was once their life, and now they're part of the past, just like the buildings. But when we see younger people — teenagers — we think, *My God, what must it be like for them to be pondering their future? They probably can't wait to get out.*

That thought got to the core of what the measurement for a healthy community needs to be: Do the youth see a future for themselves in their hometown? It also led to a statement that became a bit of a rally cry: "Imagine our kids changing the world without having to leave home."

Cities start to decline when children don't see a future for themselves in their hometown.

The Bentway Is a Better Way

SOMETIMES JOY IS FOUND BY TURNING THE WORLD UPSIDE down. That's somewhat the case with one of Toronto's newest urban parks — The Bentway. Who would have thought of looking for a new public space under an expressway? Well, Ken Greenberg did. The issues and opportunities we discuss in *The Joy Experiments* are nothing new to Ken. He led the charge on many of these topics when he was the director of Urban Design and Architecture for the City of Toronto and principal of Greenberg Consultants. If anyone is able to turn the world, and an expressway, upside down for the better, it would be Mr. Greenberg.

The Gardiner Expressway is no ordinary expressway. It's a controversial piece of urban planning created in the day and age when cities were built for the automobile first and humans second … or third. It cut most of the city off from its waterfront and still gets in the way of the natural desire to take a summer stroll along the lake. Over the years, it's represented a battle line between those who think cities should be for people and those who believe they should serve efficiency.

For much of its path through downtown Toronto, the Gardiner is elevated high overhead. Below, it's grey desolation in the form of shadows, more roads, and vacant spaces of dirt. Or is that concrete structure a natural cover from the elements — capable of suspending lights, public art, and other apparatuses that could help transform the land below into an outdoor performance space? Could the empty space that no one ventured near be a connecting space, giving people better walking access to other neighbourhood attractions and other neighbours? It turns out it can.

Today, The Bentway is a highly unique part of Toronto that offers year-round artistic, cultural, and recreational activities and events, including public art installations, seasonal and special exhibitions, theatre and musical performances, festivals, and creative marketplaces. Many people feel its uniqueness is its 1.75-kilometre-long ice-skating trail, but just as unique and perhaps more important is its "for the community by the community" process in being created.

The funding for The Bentway came from a unique public-private partnership between the City of Toronto and philanthropists Judy and Wilmot Matthews, who contributed $25 million to the project, which allowed for some experimentation that would have been difficult within a traditional funding model. A great deal of public consultation took place with neighbours, potential user groups, and creative minds that eventually brought the space to life with engaging programming, now under the control of The Bentway Conservancy, a new not-for-profit organization.

The Bentway, devoid of all the usual elements of a park, allows us to see the most important role public spaces offer us — the chance to connect to one another. §

Scott: When I first started down the path of the Creative Capital of Canada, I was mainly thinking about Waterloo Region's identity and our ability to continue to attract business and talent and build a vibrant future. There was, and still is, a strong business need for selling ourselves to the world. Attracting innovation economy talent is a bit of a bottleneck for communities of our size. But there was also another need I was feeling. A father of two young kids, I'm raising them in the community I grew up in, and while I'd be happy for them regardless of where success takes them, I'd like them to have the option of succeeding at home.

At these early stages of thought, I headed off on a family vacation to Vancouver, a city very different than my home. Vancouver isn't perfect but neither is any city. It struggles with spiralling housing costs and homelessness. But since it's surrounded by breathtaking nature, it values beauty and an active population. By "value," I mean it's prepared to spend money to make things beautiful and engaging. We strolled through the joyful area of False Creek. I took my kids to Science World, an interactive museum of sorts, whose vision is "through science and nature, we ignite wonder and empower dreams," and I watched their eyes light up to the playful joy of learning and expanding horizons. Distinctly, I recall thinking that Vancouver must really believe its youth are worth this investment. I wondered what the lack of such an institution in my own tech-and-science-oriented community said about our belief in our kids. I was determined to return home and put a strong youth focus on our Joy Experiments and the real estate work of HIP Developments.

We're blessed in Waterloo Region, since we're home to great educational institutions such as the world-renowned University of Waterloo, Wilfrid Laurier University, Conestoga College, and the Perimeter Institute. The University of Waterloo was originally created by community leaders and reflected local industries' need for engineers and other science-based graduates. That plan was so successful that today it brings top global talent to our community, and in some instances they stay and help build our economy. BlackBerry is the obvious example of that. But over time, this success has led to our community's approach to talent attraction to be best described as "transient." We count on these post-secondary schools to attract some of the best talent in the world, we hope they'll stay, and a few do. Most don't because the best talent in the world can live anywhere in the world. All in all, it works fairly well, but I feel as if we've forgotten about our own kids, and in turn, they've stopped seeing the University of Waterloo as achievable. I think the approach would be more sustainable if we had strategies to ensure the kids who grow up in the community are part of the talent-attraction plan.

One night I put it this way to myself: I see how we support the creative and entrepreneurial spirit in kids from all over the world, think it's brilliant, and don't want it to change. But we need plans and tactics for instilling the same spirit in the kids who grow up in Waterloo Region, a form of talent-building rather than relying heavily on talent-renting. We should be demonstrating that we especially want homegrown talent to succeed because we'd then have a chance to build future stakeholders in our cities. Hometown success leads to hometown investment more consistently than the common tech

It's important to mentor hometown success and celebrate it widely through the community.

start-up stories of going to school, creating a company, getting a first round of investment, selling to a tech giant, and then living somewhere else. I believe that if the community's next generation of kids understood their roots and how they're part of a community lineage that supports their success, then we'd really be city building. To that end, HIP created three youth-oriented Joy Experiments.

LAUNCH Waterloo

The first youth-oriented Joy Experiment is devoted to STEAM (science, technology, engineering, arts, math) programming for kids, which is up and running as a not-for-profit. The focus of the programming is to ensure all kids in Waterloo Region have a chance to explore and grow their creative problem-solving skills, stay curious, and connected.

The structure of the program was intentionally done to reflect and engage our broad community, even families that don't naturally gravitate to science and higher learning. LAUNCH encourages STEAM participation as a team activity in the same way as hockey. It's sort of a minor association for creativity in which kids get to experience teamwork, competitiveness, awards, and leadership. This approach also gives parents a familiar structure for volunteerism.

Two other unique experimental programs were created with the goals of

- teaching kids about the Waterloo Region creative lineage,
- building confidence in students' creative abilities, and
- making kids feel they play a role in extending the community's success.

Create30

A true grassroots approach designed to be fun and accessible, the Create30 program is pushed to the general public via social media and the Creative Capital of Canada website. But its real value is its focus on teachers, schools, and parents. Not only are there exercises designed to show kids they're creative, we also include messaging focused on the long history within Waterloo Region of everyday people creatively problem-solving and inventing things that impacted our nation and at times the world. Working to present these stories in ways that make them fun and relevant for today and tomorrow, we aren't offering them in an effort to build people's knowledge of the past. Instead, we want the stories to become tools for developing the future.

Paul: Whenever you go into Scott's office, it always seems as if he has a new book to share. More often than not the book has to do with how to expand the creative abilities of kids. I'm not sure if he's getting the books for his kids or his own mental improvement. Maybe both, and if so, that would be amazing fun. Scott showed me how these books are full of fun little exercises that help kids and people of all ages push the limits of their minds. Sometimes the ideas in these books simply help people look at the world around themselves differently, which is three-quarters of the battle toward being creative in my opinion. He said these books are like creative "workouts for the mind." They also remind him about a National Football League program called Play 60 that challenges kids to do physical exercises every day to improve their health.

With his usual enthusiasm, Scott suggested we do the same challenge approach for making kids more creatively fit or at least get them to realize they have creative abilities. I liked this language because I believe the creativity in everyone's brain is like a muscle. If you don't use it and experiment with it, it gets flabby. If you do give it regular exercise, it becomes strong and sharp. That's why some artists are always collecting weird things and making odd lampshades or furniture. That's why I'm constantly taking pictures of seemingly mundane things, exercising my creativity, keeping it strong and prepared for when it might be needed.

We brainstormed and borrowed a bunch of exercises ranging from photographing shadows to writing stories about things in the lost-and-found box. My belief was that all these fun exercises should be placed into four categories that reflect how creative minds naturally work. In other words, four exercise groups to strengthen the "imagination muscle" we all have but often don't use. Here's what creative people do all the time:

- **Observing:** Creative people are really good at looking at the world around them and noticing interesting everyday things most of us forget to see ... like shadows or the different shapes of trees.
- **Changing Perspectives:** Creative people not only observe life all the time, they also try to change how they see things to help put new importance on these objects. Maybe they imagine what things would look like if they were short like a dog. Or maybe they try to imagine what a telephone pole would say if it could talk and had feelings. It might be concerned about that short dog coming up the street.
- **Super Play:** Creative people will grab things and start mixing and matching just to see what happens. They may not even have any idea what they're trying to create, but they enjoy seeing what happens when you add, subtract, or turn things upside down. Super play is all about open experimenting. It's like starting a story with a sentence and then turning to friends and asking them, "And then what?," hoping they can continue the story. Then doing that over and over until they can hardly believe the story they've written. It can be fun not having a goal and just seeing what happens.

- **Fail Well:** Creative people know there's always something to learn when we fail at doing things. And what we learn could be the most important step in inventing something new. Creative people aren't scared of failing. They don't say "I failed." They say, "The idea failed, but now I'm a step closer to succeeding." They know that if they keep trying, the failures will eventually help them succeed.

Meander STEAM Curriculum

The third experiment for kids is a wonderful spin-off of *Meander*, the living architecture sculpture now in place at Gaslight Square in Cambridge. While not quite as accessible as Create30, the *Meander* STEAM Curriculum offers kids the opportunity to experience some of the most refined hands-on STEAM learning in the world.

The *Meander* program is an almost perfect symbol of what STEAM education and thinking are all about. Developed in conjunction with local teacher participation, it offers schools an in-class study structure and a field trip for students in which the *Meander* sculpture acts as a visual inspiration and teaching tool. The program was expressly created for Grades 5 and 8 students and promotes their engagement and learning of standards-based content and vital higher-level thinking skills. It's based on how systems such as the Grand River and *Meander* constantly change and reorganize.

In the program, students are asked to solve how to minimize heavy flooding on the Grand using an aesthetically pleasing sculpture. The activities integrate science, visual art, and language with important thinking skills such as problem-solving, changing perspectives, synthesizing, and envisioning.

Students get to bring the science, art, writing, and oral communication skills they've acquired in their schooling and lives to the *Meander* field trip experience to facilitate success in their problem-solving task.

Scott: We devote all of Chapter 10 to *Meander*, the largest permanent living architecture sculpture in the world, part of HIP's Gaslight Square project in Cambridge, Ontario, because it influences so much of our Joy Experiments perspective. When we first considered Philip Beesley's work for Gaslight, it was primarily about creating a cool visual experience that could reflect some of the dreamy aspects of nature and the Grand River. It certainly does that. But with Philip's help we also started to see it as a brilliant representation of STEAM learning, which we were already supporting with LAUNCH, as well as what nature can teach us about problem-solving, sustainable architecture, and even economics.

Considering our community's creative problem-solving lineage, we wanted the *Meander* program to become a destination for people wanting to truly immerse themselves in a new perspective and process for solving the challenges that lie ahead of humanity. We especially wanted it to be a destination for the schools and children of Waterloo Region.

Philip and team were very enthusiastic, and through their network of STEAM educators and thought leaders, they were able to bring to the

Celebrated hometown success leads to future hometown city builders who invest in their city's future.

table Lucinda Presley of the Institute of Creativity Empowering Education (ICEE) Success Foundation in Washington, D.C., and Rob Gorbet of the Living Architecture Systems Group in Waterloo.

Create30 and the *Meander* program connect with our youth directly. They build confidence in their creativity and attach that confidence to Waterloo Region's creative lineage, ensuring it's alive and well by fostering the next generation's success. Within that activity, there's a model for every city: mentor hometown success, spread it widely throughout the community, celebrate it, and watch it grow. You can see this model work within the American college system: heavy mentoring, celebrating, and almost tribal-like community building with the result of tremendous loyalty and financial giveback by graduates.

I believe developing a confident and inclusive community identity is as much about city building as condos and office towers are, otherwise I wouldn't be investing so much of myself into these experiments. Cities need something to unify their human energy and passion, especially in these divisive and challenging times. Sometimes it's hard for us to see commonality in one another. And when asked to give to a cause, many people reply, "What do I get back?" But it seems easier to get buy-in and support when the focus of identity is shifted to our youth and the next generation of our communities. Sometimes it's easier to invest in the future than in the present.

These programs are built in an open way; there's lots of room for other groups and individuals to step in and grow the activity through leadership or sponsorship. That's part of the goal of Joy Experiments: if they work and catch the imagination of others, they don't stay experiments for very long. They become the bedrock of change.

Making your mark.

CHAPTER NINE

Experimental Journeys

Eliminating Old Ideas that Obstruct New Ones

With the Creative Capital of Canada community identity experiment, we outlined a Joy Experiment that didn't have the results we hoped for or expected. Some would call it a failed experiment. We call it a success because we see experiments as journeys. So having said that semi-confusing statement, now seems as good a time as any to discuss the need, importance, and structure of experimentation.

Let's start with need. Throughout this book, we make the case that the context in which large and mid-sized cities operate is transforming due to the effects of Covid-19, climate change, the long-term global population migration toward urban centres, and the digital economy. Cities have always played a major role in economics, politics, the arts, and social interaction. And so, as the world changes, it's hard to conceive urban centres not drastically doing so, as well. The rate of change is going to increase as some cities meet these challenges with adaptation and adjustments of their own. Andy Burnham, mayor of Greater Manchester, England, eloquently stated that future cities will be designed to be enjoyed. That's certainly music to our ears. The "super cities" of the world will unquestionably continue to solidify their positions as the places where inventive minds congregate to PLAY, LIVE, WORK.

So where does that leave mid-sized cities? Continuing with the status quo seems inconceivable.

An example of a city meeting change with change is Calgary, Alberta. That city's former mayor, Naheed Nenshi, saw the future of his city as moving from a place to work to being a place to live. The city created a new vision

> **Change is being thrust upon cities and must be met with change. Status quo is the biggest of risk of all.**

articulated as "A great place to make a living. A great place to make a life." With that strategic focus, it marketed its tech sector with surprisingly different ads. Those ads hit close to home for us because Calgary actually placed billboards with them in Waterloo Region. *Ouch!*

Calgary's commitment to change isn't just a collection of powerful words and ads. The city's new central library is a shining commitment to … dare we say … *joy!* Everything about the building, notably location and programming, was designed to disrupt the old notions of the city and create a shared sense of a vibrant community. It's unfair to think of the structure as just a library of books. Its mandate is to be a broader educational centre, offering learning labs, residency programs, and digital production studios. The library is organized in terms of "fun to serious" as you ascend its stairs. *Time* magazine included the new Calgary library in its 2019 greatest places list. It's a stunning and happy piece of architecture and programming.

But Calgary is just one example that can be heralded to prove the race to a PLAY, LIVE, WORK community is on and the business of city building is already shifting. As a result, applying the usual goals, processes, and criteria to city planning and avoiding risk will become the biggest gamble of all. The primary reason why "the usual" will no longer work is because most of the existing rules and perspectives were created during a long period of stability in which consistency and the prevention of bad things happening was highly valued. In fact, bad things not happening was a form of win!

Paul: At one point in my career, I learned a valuable lesson. I worked for a very large insurance company and saw how some people were able to advance in their careers without big-project successes being attached to their names. I equated success with change and new initiatives, but what I learned, somewhat painfully, was that success inside organizations that were doing okay was equated with the absence of bad things happening.

Anyone acting as a change agent will have both successes and failures as part of their track records. Quite simply there's risk in change. Organizations sailing in calm waters tend to reward people who avoid having bad things happen on their watches. They may not be the ones who make great things happen, but they never make anything bad happen.

But eventually the external world changes and the waters are no longer calm. Change must be met with change. In these moments, organizations head outside their offices in search of consultants who can lead them to innovation and a risk-free "eureka" leap. Risk-free innovation sounds delightful, doesn't it?

It probably doesn't need to be stated, but for the record, my inclination toward creativity led to zero promotions in that company. But I'm not bitter … much.

It's a certainty that the future will be a very different place, and while controlling risk is a good thing, avoiding it at all cost will most certainly lead to disaster.

Scott: When it comes to city building, a lot of people think of pilot projects as the ideal way to mitigate risk. But I've witnessed too many pilots that really become self-fulfilling failures. Over and over, I see communities wanting to try something new such as … bike lanes. Right out of the gate, they attempt to keep things contained and fund the activity with small budgets because, well, it's just a pilot, after all. So they set up a short section of lanes that begin nowhere in particular and end with a similar destination. Projects like this have such little impact on people's lives that the results aren't impressive, and the conclusion is that bike lanes are a bad idea, which may or may not be true. In an effort to minimize financial and obligational risks, there's nothing really learned in these pilot projects. There's no risk and no forward movement. That's not what we mean when we talk about experimentation. This is the "no man's land" of innovation. People want brilliant new ideas and desperately try to get there without risk, which also means without learning.

We all have Calgary Central Library dreams. Surely, there's a way … somehow. When the risk-free path isn't obvious, we sometimes replace it with the stuttering of risk aversion in which organizations stumble in circles rather than move forward. And here's the really hard part: creative experts, even Thomas Edison in his day, will tell you that eureka moments are a myth. Quoting again from *How to Fly a Horse* by Kevin Ashton, "The creativity myth implies that few people can be creative, that any successful creator will experience dramatic flashes of insight, and that creating is more like magic than work." People want to believe in magic because it eliminates risk. Magic never fails. But the myth is just that — a story that's simply not true.

So if standing still is the ultimate risk in changing times and eureka doesn't exist, what are we to do?

There are no leaps to innovation, but there are ways of walking toward new ideas. Ashton states: "The best artists, scientists, engineers, inventors, entrepreneurs and other creators are the ones who keep taking steps by finding new problems, new solutions, and then new problems again." It's a left-foot problem, right-foot solution approach. The structure innovators use to take these steps is experimentation, whereby they question why something isn't working and what ingredient needs to change to make it work.

The innovation cities need to achieve, be it bike lanes or world-renowned libraries, occurs by working through all the options — usually eliminating things that don't work until arriving at the right combination. In this process, finding what doesn't work is actually a success because it eliminates an old idea, perception, or

OK
Good 'Nuf
PREDICTABLE
Done!
same
OLD
THIS IS IT.

belief that's likely blocking the ability to see a new way of doing things. Risk is mitigated by a process that views things not working out as an important step forward. Failure only occurs when we stop trying or learning.

Returning to Chapter 7 and our search for how to get a community to celebrate identity, we noted that traditional methods of committees, logos, and slogans weren't getting our community any closer to success. But people continued trying those methods, hoping for a different outcome. That's failure because the old ideas were obstructing everyone's ability to see new ones.

Having witnessed the problem, we developed the idea that perhaps a social movement and celebration were better than a committee boardroom. That was a left-foot problem to a right-foot possible solution moment. It was an important step forward. We built a movement using a few new tools we saw at our disposal such as populist techniques that held potential based on the examples of other cities. That didn't work. Failure? No, not in the creative experimental journey method. Our step eliminated a wrong idea from our sight that allowed us to see the importance of engaging the community in ways that were more in line with its behavioural DNA. Once again: left-foot problem followed by right-foot solution. Maybe we're at the solution, or perhaps we have a few more steps to take. But one thing is certain: we're closer to success and a long way away from debating a tagline.

The most important thing experimentation offers is momentum and the elimination of old, obsolete ideas, which allows people to place themselves in a new context with new tools. It changes the discussion, and that can change everything.

The no-man's-land issue of innovation mentioned earlier was perfectly illustrated when we attended a global city-building conference that included an impressive list of experts. One of the hot topics on the agenda was the concept of the 15-minute city. It's not really a new idea, but it's taken on heightened importance in the age of climate change and Covid-19. The vision behind the 15-minute city is that everything you need should be within a 15-minute walk or bike ride of your home, regardless of the size of the city — sort of a series of micro-towns within cities.

There are no giant leaps to innovation. It's a process of taking steps.

The Better Block

THE SKEPTIC'S FAVOURITE RALLY CRY IS "PROVE IT." AT THE VERY least, it's a great stall tactic and sometimes, as in the case of city building, you can't prove it without doing it. In instances such as that, the cost of proving it often ensures nothing happens. Victory for the skeptics … until the Better Block project came along.

Better Block, from Dallas, Texas, is one of our favourite joy examples from around the world because it really grabs hold of the experimentation philosophy, the belief in city building and joy, and runs with it to the finish line and beyond.

Started in 2010 by Jason Roberts and Andrew Howard, Better Block has found a unique way to respond to "prove it." It usually involves saying "Okay, give me a week," and the next thing, they're helping communities transform grey streets and ignored parts of cities into spaces that give people joy. Better Block's website says it "educates, equips, and empowers communities and their leaders to reshape and reactivate built environments to promote the growth of healthy and vibrant neighborhoods."

That might sound fairly run-of-the-mill, but the organization's tactics are anything but. Better Block has been described as "guerrilla street redesign" and bordering on civil disobedience. In reality, the truth lies somewhere between those radical descriptions and its mission. What they really do is help communities circumvent the bureaucratic barriers, rules, ordinances, laws, and empty budgets that keep neighbourhoods from turning into the types of places we love to visit around the world.

Better Block creates living experiments (*charette* for our architect and planning friends) cheaply, quickly, and with no permanent infrastructure. Bike lanes appear using tape and paint that washes away in the rain. Streets give birth to green boulevards with the help of hay bales and shrubs on loan from local nurseries. Parking lots become enjoyable parkettes thanks to wooden skids and sounds created by local musicians. Almost instantly these experiments create instant feedback and an army of new advocates for change. Sometimes officials show up and say, "You can't do this," but Better Block does and people love the joy that results. And that kind of proof makes progress a whole lot easier.

The Better Block project started in Jason Roberts's hometown of Dallas and a four-block area in the Oak Cliff neighbourhood full of empty streets. The city had a number of laws on the books that prevented the area from ever becoming more than what it was. There was even a law that prevented people from congregating. Within 24 hours, and with the help of friends, Jason was able to transform the area into a sea of greenery, cafés, and play areas. It was hard for officials to deny that it could be done, that people would come, and that perhaps some rules needed to be changed.

Today, Better Block helps communities around the world, from Australia to Iran, and it even brought its skills to a stretch of Danforth Avenue in Toronto and proved people were willing to give up a few parking spots for a few parkettes (see betterblock.org). §

The experts viewed the challenges to moving toward the 15-minute city goal in Herculean terms. They stated that a 15-minute city couldn't be achieved until cities abandon planning policies that intentionally segregate themselves into residential/retail/industrial areas. Another expert suggested that social segregation needed to change for the 15-minute city to be achieved. Yet another pointed out that reliance on the automobile had to be completely overturned. All of these statements are true to one degree or another. But they're also so big that the simple concept people were hoping for became overwhelming. Considering most organizations' desire to mitigate risk, the effect of these pronouncements actually turned people away from the goal rather than encouraging action.

One attendee asked if there were any small steps that could be considered. The long pause from the experts was very telling. Clearly, everyone at the conference, both experts and attendees, were struggling for superhuman leaps to match the colossal challenges that had been outlined. Instead of searching for the eureka, we should have been looking for the journey of experiments that would get us ever closer to the goal.

Scott: Embracing the experimental approach to building the future of mid-sized cities is critical. Change is upon us, and there will soon be big winners and losers. Experiments can be large or small, but they're all steps forward if they're set up with a belief in success and a willingness to learn from shortfalls. I believe mid-sized cities have an advantage over big cities in this area. Collaboration and the sharing of risk between the private and public sectors is easier to achieve in cities that aren't huge. And smaller experiments can have bigger impacts in mid-sized cities.

I'm admittedly a bigger gambler than some people, but I do my homework and set expectations for our experiments, accepting that experimentation is a journey of steps. I believe cities that are built for enjoyment are well worth the journey. The term *Joy Experiments* uses two words that have equal importance to us. Joy can't be accomplished without experiments.

Eliminate things that don't work such as old ideas, perceptions, and beliefs. Those things block our ability to see new ways of doing things.

Sunday journeys.

CHAPTER TEN

There Is Nothing Wrong with a Big Idea

Experimentation, even at a small level, can have significant positive results. It keeps the wheels of progress rolling and has a way of gathering supportive followers. Experimentation can change conversations from "We can't do that because we aren't a big city" to "Well maybe ..." and eventually to "We don't have to do it like a big city. We can to it in our own unique way. *But we have to do it!*"

At the same time, there's also nothing wrong with a big idea.

We don't believe big ideas are always measured by their price tags or the volume of noise they make. The best measure of a big idea is the number of threads within it that connect to other ideas or events. We've talked about how some experiments don't work out as planned and that those setbacks can still have a positive effect through the elimination of wrong ideas that block the view of better thoughts. Big-idea experiments can also assist our vision by extending their influence in a way that allows us to see patterns and themes within our community's cultural fabric that might have been overlooked.

As you read through *The Joy Experiments*, you'll have come across several mentions of the living architecture sculpture *Meander*. This piece of public art has influenced a lot of our other Joy Experiments, but that wasn't the intention when we first pondered Philip Beesley's work. Thankfully, we were willing to keep the windows of our minds open for a little extra joy to enter. *Meander*'s impact helped us make other Joy Experiments better and bigger. It also added a fluid quality to our plans. That's

important because people, cultures, dare we say cities, are dynamic. They shift, change, and can be rebuilt in unique ways.

Paul: I discovered Philip Beesley's living architecture sculpture work while researching examples of how my "Creative Intersections" public space strategy could work in Waterloo Region. I needed to illustrate how the world-class thinking in Waterloo Region could come out from behind the walls of institutions and "play in public." I needed to show how that type of content could advance the community's cultural understanding of itself.

The "Creative Intersections" strategy contained a formula for transforming world-class content into animated entertainment via collaborations between the community's organizations and the talents of installation artists. It's worth stressing that while "Creative Intersections" is certainly about learning, most importantly it's about fun and celebration. The ultimate goal of the "Creative Intersections" strategy was to reintroduce the community to itself in a way that would encourage a unique and tangible vibe on the streets of Waterloo Region.

The Creative Intersections Formula.

I was searching for a way to demonstrate "Creative Intersections" in downtown Cambridge along the Grand River that included the University of Waterloo's School of Architecture, situated in that area. It seemed the obvious place to explore in the hope of finding some world-class talent and content to introduce to the broader community. As I scanned websites and talked to people, I came upon Philip Beesley, a faculty member at the school and the creator of interactive living architecture sculptures that look very much like plant life but are anything but that. I was pleasantly surprised to learn that his work had been exhibited all over the world. And yet, as is so often the case, no one locally knew anything about what he was creating right under their noses.

Admittedly, I didn't know the full implications of his work but had a sense it could create a dreamy experience for people to think about the Grand River that cuts right through the city but lacked folklore. My wish was that local world-class content could reintroduce the community to its own river.

That storytelling deficit was made painfully clear to me one day when I walked around downtown Cambridge while working on the Gaslight District project for Scott. One block from the river was a well-executed mural of two children

> **Big ideas have the power to connect to other ideas and events. They push our perspectives and help us see opportunities we hadn't considered.**

gazing at the ocean and a whale breaching. At that moment, I thought about the stories we never tell about our community, and here I was faced with an artifact that celebrated someone else's water. I wondered: *Do we have to borrow imagery from somewhere else to be inspired?* I really wanted that to change via Philip's work. That hint of what I thought was a significant idea was just the beginning of the journey big ideas can take us on.

Before we really understood how big an idea *Meander* was to become, we had an opportunity to physically and emotionally feel it. During the discussion and negotiation that led to HIP commissioning Philip, he opened a large installation of his work at the Royal Ontario Museum (ROM) in Toronto. Having not really seen his work in person, we drove down the highway to see living architecture in action, and the experience was highly enlightening.

On any given weekday, the ROM is full of school kids running noisily from dinosaurs to mummies and back again. That energy infects the whole museum, so it was surprising to notice the strong change in behaviour when people entered the living architecture spaces housed on the upper floors. Dashing about changed to slow walking or simply standing still. The noisy chattering found in every other hall was reduced to whispers. People quietly wandered about, reaching toward the sculpture to see how its motion sensors would react to their presence with sounds, lights, and motions of its own. No one was in a hurry to get to the next exhibit, since they were experiencing a representation of nature in a new and very interactive way. The mood was one of reverence.

Scott: At the ROM, I stood with my head in the middle of one of the sculpture's spheres. It chirped, flashed, and hummed as it reacted to me being so close. Quickly, I was informed by security that I had to step away, but no matter, the decision was made. At that moment, I knew we simply had to make this happen back home. This work was conceived and built by Philip and the Living Architecture Systems Group, a Waterloo Region–based collective of artists, architects, engineers, software developers, and scientists. The people back home needed to learn that this, too, was what their community was about. This would be an imaginative way to contemplate their own river. And the security guard needed to calm down.

Before going any further, perhaps it's best to let Philip Beesley describe *Meander*:

> The initial conversations with Scott Higgins and Paul Kalbfleisch focused on the possibility of installing a large work of public art that might anchor the spaces of Tapestry Hall, a historic building that acts as a centrepiece of the Gaslight development. *Meander* was conceived to work directly with the architectural vision and surrounding lands. The interior courtyard spaces of the historic Gaslight manufacturing complex opened up to a continuous riverside landscape. Within that interconnected new public space, the vast timber-framed reaches of Tapestry Hall formed a centre, opening its new atrium to the public in openings reaching north and south. The crossing point within that interior space became the focus of my explorations with Scott and Paul.
>
> Working with several collaborators — the mechatronics engineer and artist Rob Gorbet at the University of Waterloo, sound artist Salvador Breed, and many other computational scientists and creative designers — we conceived of a suspended sculpture environment that would reach to public open areas and deep within the reaches of the main hall inside. Undulating layers were conceived arching and billowing overhead within the sculpture, seeking to embody the spirit of the meandering Grand River. The work now forms a great hovering canopy containing clouds of gentle lightweight material, floating and reaching up and down and through the space. Within the centre of that canopy is a deeply interwoven grotto containing intricate lace-like hemispherical nests and hollows. Surrounding that centre within the larger suspended cloud are river-like meshwork surfaces that reach up high, arcing around mezzanines that allow the public to walk up and around and through the material.
>
> As a work of public art, *Meander* now serves as a transformed place that expands the possibilities of architecture and sculpture by interweaving active electronics, sound, light, motion, and chemistry. *Meander* contains a custom-control system containing dozens of miniature computers located in clusters throughout the river-shaped canopies and central grotto-like cores. When viewers move and gesture within the sculpture, it responds with ripples of soft waving motions of fronds and glowing lights and whispers of sound, as well. The effect is of a deeply involved animated experience.

As we worked with Philip, we slowly began to understand the inner workings of living architecture and the visions in his mind. Living architecture was a purposeful blending of science, technology, engineering, art, and math, or STEAM — the new form of problem-solving learning being taught in some schools. This interrelated approach to observing situations and solving problems was the only possible way to create something that expresses the intricacies of nature because nature itself is an interrelated web of systems. When that penny dropped in our minds, the first significant thread of *Meander* reached out and touched another Joy Experiment — LAUNCH, one of HIP's earliest experiments involving a non-profit start-up venture to create and curate STEAM-powered programming to harness the creativity and curiosity of Waterloo Region's youngest citizens.

The more we talked about the living architecture sculpture project, the more we saw it as the ultimate visual expression of STEAM. Its power was so strong we knew that any kid experiencing it would be excited to get involved in STEAM learning. We also realized that *Meander* was more than an expression of the Grand River; it was the symbol and expression of Waterloo Region's problem-solving future. New discussions quickly got underway to develop a learning curriculum to align with LAUNCH and support local school field trips to *Meander* so that kids could immerse themselves in a new way of observing the world around them.

The name *Meander* even began to take on multiple meanings. Initially, the inspiration came from the shape of the Grand River, a slow-moving, twisting oxbow channel of water that runs through Southern Ontario. It weaves and meanders. But it also fitted perfectly with the idea that the power of STEAM comes from the blending of science, technology, engineering, art, and math. STEAM isn't about learning more about each subject in silos. It focuses on processing problems through those subjects to arrive at robust and sustainable solutions.

Meander started being installed at Tapestry Hall in December 2019. With one-quarter of its massive skeletal frame hanging high above us, we wondered out loud, "What have we done?" It was a comment made partially in jest, but there was also a bit of honesty to the comment. It was so big, so impressive, and exceeded our expectations.

Scott: What we'd done was much more than commission a sculpture or integrate it with the school STEAM curriculum. We'd put the PLAY + LIVE + WORK = JOY formula in motion. Philip's work and the *Meander* experience, so beautifully displayed at Tapestry Hall, playfully engages the public with spectacle and motion. In very short order, the sculpture and its surroundings has become a place that changes the way people dream about their city. It makes them believe big things can happen here. *Meander* will influence how we as a community live. Whether it's through school programs, pillow nights when the public is invited to lie on the floor and stare up at all that brilliance, or as a wedding backdrop, *Meander* shifts the character of our daily lives in an enthusiastic way. And as a symbol of STEAM

and the future of problem-solving, *Meander* will support the next generation of Waterloo Region's thinkers, creators, and inventors. It's emblematic of the creative dynamism and the technological and artistic leadership and potential of this community.

The best and most important part of big ideas is they tend not to respect the traditional boundaries of our thinking. Big ideas shift perspectives and make people view things differently, even if that's a bit uncomfortable at first. They can also change the context of plans and connect things in a way that makes everything bigger.

In other words, big ideas have an organic quality to them, and if the objective is a city that offers joy, then every so often a big idea needs to be tossed into the mix of experiments because joy is also fluid.

Meander was more than an expression of the Grand River; it was the symbol and expression of Waterloo Region's problem-solving future.

The layers of a day in the city.

Culturally Ambitious Bristol

FROM ITS HISTORY IN THE EARLY 20TH CENTURY AS A MAJOR port, aircraft manufacturing hub, and collection of textile mills, Bristol, England, has come a long way. With the help of its two universities, it's evolved into the country's second-largest digital economic centre and can brag at a global level about its impressive technology and creative talent pool making businesses consider relocating to the city. That in itself is an impressive story, and so is the fact that it's the home of Banksy! Who knew? But more impressive than either of those claims are the plans the city has for its future.

Bristol understands that culture is more than a tool for improving the quality of life. The city sees it as a key economic driver of its future. Bristol's leaders have realized that industries based on creativity and knowledge, and the subsequent creation of innovative ideas, is its best route to become a sustainable city. That means leaving past economic models based on factories and the Avon River in the past. The future is a whole new ball game, and this city is prepared to play in a whole new way. In the innovation economy, money follows talent, and talent is attracted to inspiration and energy. Bristol has made the amazing link between those realities and the value of building a city full of joy, even to the point where it plans on creating spaces for spontaneity.

The city's commitment to a radically different economic development plan is impressive. Back in 2011, Bristol already had a sizable list of cultural amenities but still made a long-term commitment to outdo potential competition and become "culturally ambitious." The goal it set was to turn Bristol's cultural organizations and creative industries into a world-class economic asset. Today, culture is Bristol's ace in the hole. It's been ranked the best place to live in the United Kingdom in terms of wealth and happiness. Bristol businesses brag to new recruits that there's plenty to do in the city — much of it in public, much of it free. We suggest you check out visitbristol.co.uk to understand the size of the city's commitment to joyful moments.

This kind of goal and success can't be achieved by city hall alone. It requires the commitment and collaboration of all sectors of the community and economy. In 2019, city leaders developed the Bristol Culture Standards, a set of pledges around best employment and working practice in arts and culture. Organizations and employers, both private and public and in the cultural sector, have been invited to sign on and maintain these standards in their work environments. Since this was part of the city's effort to build a collaborative and inclusive strategy for cultural support, the document itself was drafted through a "co-writing" process.

Clearly, Bristol is serious about its ambitions. §

CHAPTER ELEVEN

Fifty Bright Ideas Are Better Than One

In the software industry, the term *open source* describes products with publicly accessible code such as Linux. As a philosophy, open source is a collaboration that can go beyond being a tactic to achieve bigger and quicker success. Sometimes broad collaboration and alignment are the end goals rather than just the means. *The Joy Experiments* is an example of that type of activity and vision. The goal of the book is to create a common discussion about city building accessible to politicians, architects, citizens, city planners, real estate developers, and social agencies. It has a single focus that affects all of us — the infrastructure for the human spirit (joy). As authors, we seek to create a collaborative audience of people willing to discuss what they want from the communities they live and work in. We don't propose to know or control the outcomes of those discussions, and the experiments we share aren't necessarily right or relevant for everyone. We merely want to set the table for a better form of city-building ecosystem, one very much needed for a challenging future.

The popular folklore of invention often tells the story of the isolated individual madly working away on an idea the rest of the world thinks is crazy. This is the Steve Jobs tale in his parents' garage with the door closed and most certainly locked. But open-source behaviour, as we like to call it, runs counter to this narrative. It might still involve a garage, and the world might still believe the idea is crazy, but in our new story the garage door is open, discussion takes place with others, and perhaps the brightest idea of all is the light that spills out of the garage onto the street, attracting others to participate with their doors open.

Scott: I'm proud of Waterloo Region, my home. We're a community that for the most part has managed to avoid getting stuck in a rut while the world around us has changed. The deindustrialization of North America closed many of our factories, but we successfully evolved into an information-and-innovation economy. When Paul and I were researching the long-past business successes of our community, it was shocking to realize that almost all these companies no longer existed. They were part of a golden era of industry that's now gone. Yet here we're still succeeding with new businesses, new names, and new inventions.

One of the main reasons for our ability to evolve is due to the way this community collaborates. People are generous with ideas and support. In Waterloo Region, they're happy to share their network contacts from their smartphones. If you have a business problem, they'll connect you to someone who might have the answer or be a valuable long-term mentor. If I have a new idea I'm working on, I've always found it easy to find others to add to my thoughts and help it grow.

This form of generosity dates back to the early 1900s when local businesses that might naturally have competed against one another also found ways to collaborate in an effort to make the community more internationally competitive. It's a gritty and determined form of collaboration that perhaps goes back even farther to our Mennonite barn-raising traditions.

There isn't a lot of literal barn-raising going on these days, but perhaps the most dynamic, modern-day equivalent of that idea is the open-source movement. In the software industry, *open source* applies to products with publicly

Collaboration can help achieve individual success quicker.

accessible code. Anyone can see the code, adapt it, and share it however they want.

One of the goals of open-source software is to build an ecosystem of success rather than a single stand-alone product success, which is an appropriate description of the type of collaboration we describe so often in this book. It's the acknowledgement that we can achieve more and get farther ahead when we share ideas and effort. I personally experience this form of collaboration among my real estate development competitors in the community. We compete head to head when it comes to acquiring land, but after that point, a lot of thoughts and ideas get shared over lunches, emails, and phone calls because the success of one property leads to more interest in the community and more opportunities.

Paul: I suspect this form of collaboration can be found in a lot of mid-sized cities. It may take shape in different ways as it addresses different issues, but the beauty of a mid-sized city is that it has a scale that allows, or forces, you to see and respect the people around you. I brought my consulting business to Waterloo Region because of a project that allowed me to shape strategy around community culture. My hope was that once I succeeded with that project, I'd get similar ones in other cities. But to my surprise the project led to more and more related work in this community. That happened because I was bumping into people and my projects kept overlapping other activities. It grew enough to make an impact that I could measure.

There are a lot of people like me who have learned the secret advantage of places smaller than super cities. Don't get me wrong. I still love going to New York City and soaking up every bit of incredible inspiration. I simply can't get enough of that big-city vitality. But within my community, I get something that's perhaps more important. I'm able to get buy-in, participation, collaboration, and opportunities for co-creation on everything from developing unique street corners to public spaces and art. For me, co-creation is the product.

The dynamic scale of a mid-sized city is what makes their stories so interesting. For example, since the 1970s, Winnipeg, Manitoba, has been diligently transforming an old section of its downtown core into a lively urban centre while at the same time preserving an impressive collection of early-20th-century office buildings created in the Chicago architecture style. I've visited this area, now known as the Exchange District, and think it's one of the coolest urban neighbourhoods I know because it feels real and gentrification is somewhat held in check. I especially loved the bike lanes painted as murals, some with Freddie Mercury's lyrics about riding his bike where he likes. But what's most impressive is that this constant evolution is driven by members of the private and public sectors, as well as by citizens.

Over the years, they've formed and reformed planning groups and reworked visions for the Exchange District. The most recent collaborative plan was developed in the 1990s. They don't always get it perfect, especially since the current guiding principles are 30 years old. However, a new collaborative invention process has started. Its goal is to shape a new long-term vision for the future of this slightly rough yet totally unique 20-block area of abandoned warehouses. If you want a vital and collaborative streetscape, you need a process to match. Go Winnipeg!

Open-source behaviour can be applied to issues far more fundamental to cities than neighbourhood planning. They can, as in the case of Indianapolis, Indiana, set the course of a city's economy.

Like many Midwest North American cities, Indianapolis's industrial base turned to rust in the 1970s. Rather than assuming the community's economic ecosystem was someone else's job to run (i.e., the government) or perhaps no one's job, a combination of private and public sector leaders went in search of a new path into the future. This led to some success in becoming a centre for professional sports management, but a more robust vision was required to build sustainable prosperity for the whole region.

In the late 1990s, the Central Indiana Corporate Partnership (CICP) was formed. It included a limited set of CEOs and presidents of leading area companies, social foundations, and universities. To quote the book *The New Localism*, a CICP document, "CICP was intentionally structured to be the region's premier strategic economic arm for community leadership, providing oversight and guidance for our key business, university and philanthropic leaders, helping to prioritize resource allocation and leverage investment into those programs and institutions that could best advance regional development."

Interestingly, the group's members couldn't send substitutes to meetings. The CEOs had to be present. The CICP meant business! And while the group worked closely with politicians, public sector representation wasn't allowed. This group worked in a non-partisan fashion and mapped out an economic action plan that wasn't restricted by two- or four-year election terms.

By moving from competitors or complete strangers into collaborators and ecosystem builders, CICP created five initiatives that focused on regional strengths and drove talent and investment. Collaborative research uncovered economic assets that in the previous fragmented approaches were virtually hiding in plain sight. With data-informed plans in place and organized collaboration among the private and civic sectors, local governments were able to create an effective supporting role in this new economic ecosystem. Through this approach, Indianapolis has become a leader in biotech and equally strong in other sectors.

These are the stories of people thinking beyond a single success and acknowledging that sometimes goals can only be achieved by influencing a much larger group of people. In a world of interconnected problems, this is the form of collaboration becoming more and more relevant, especially as it relates to the topic of environmental sustainability. If we don't all eventually get on board, then success is impossible. We'd like to offer the story of a Joy Experiment, *From Behind the Mask*, to illustrate the shift in definition of the word *collaboration* from "tactic" to "goal."

From Behind the Mask

NOT LONG AGO, WE WATCHED A SEED OF JOY GROW IN OUR HOME community of Waterloo Region. *From Behind the Mask* is a great social and artistic experiment and installation. We love it so much we asked its creator, Brenda Reid, to explain it. We're also happy to say that *From Behind the Mask* is the first official recipient of the Joy Experiments Award of Merit. Congratulations, Brenda, and take it away.

"When the pandemic started, I was partway through my master of architecture program focusing on community well-being. I wanted to know how an architect could bring quality to all residents' lives through public space. I became very interested in the word *care* and how undervalued and surprisingly complicated it is. It deals with uncomfortable subject matter and always involves a power imbalance. An architect has a lot of power — the lines we draw become buildings that will affect generations of people. So how does an architect practise care for the public through work? How can we build joy in our community?

"In the summer of 2020, a few months into our 'new normal,' I spent a lot of time wandering the streets and photographing the signs of support people made in their windows, sidewalks, and front yards. I wanted to capture them before they were taken down or the rain washed them away. I was also analyzing quilts around this time, looking at their making, community, and ability to deal with painful topics. They're artifacts of care. These two things — the community reaching out to one another and quilts — clicked in my brain. What if we made a community quilt so we could tell and preserve our coronavirus stories?

"Our community quilt is made up of individual quilt blocks, allowing people to create a small part of the quilt from the safety of their home. Each block is the shape and size of a face mask. Masks have become a symbol of our care and the means of separating ourselves from one another. *From Behind the Mask* gave people the opportunity to create double-sided quilt blocks that told a part of their pandemic story. The blocks are untraditional and tie together. The spaces between the blocks represent our space between each other. The ties that hold all the blocks together represent our essential social ties — the ties of a community.

"The grounding idea for this quilt was for it to make space — physical space — for our stories of pain, resilience, and care. Everyone has had a unique experience of the pandemic within our community. This quilt-making project became a way for people to see themselves in a community-built architecture. My goal was to create this quilt to connect people to another's perspective and lived experience, to validate our differences and similarities. Together, we're building empathetic space for each other by assembling the quilt. Over 550 stories have been submitted, carefully sewn by community members and tied together to make community space. I have so many different emotions standing in front of this 25-foot-long quilt, one of which is undoubtedly joy." §

> **[The real estate development industry isn't exactly a hotbed of innovation. The business model hasn't changed in decades.]**

Scott: Like a lot of parents, I wonder and worry about what kind of world my children and grandchildren will inherit. I know we all have these thoughts, and the concern is compounded by the frustration of feeling that our individual action doesn't measure up to the challenges facing us and the seeming impossibility of change. We ask ourselves, "What can I do?" Well, in my case that question hit hard when I read that buildings account for 40 percent of North America's carbon emissions, largely from heating sources burning fossil fuels. With that data point, I felt I had little choice but to decide that HIP would build a condominium that didn't contribute to this problem. Fully electric buildings exist in Europe, and there's a lot of change taking place in California on this front, both at construction and legislative levels.

I started off by doing what I usually do when faced with a challenge. I read a lot and soon found that the possibility of a clean all-electric condo was achievable. This was followed by two years of HIP working with a design team to explore how to leverage new advancements in building electrification technology. It was encouraging to discover that new heating and cooling products could operate at a similar cost to fossil-fuel solutions when incorporated into a unique building construction envelope. This then turned into a unique Joy Experiment called the Bright Building, a 19-storey, 228-unit condominium in Kitchener that's Ontario's first all-electric high-rise residential project that will be sustainably efficient well beyond current building codes.

As I gained more knowledge, I also quickly realized that HIP's contribution to the cause had to go beyond one building. Real estate is roughly 70 percent of city-building activity. So, if our whole industry doesn't evolve, then neither will cities. HIP had to start a trend. But how do you do that in an industry that doesn't face pressure to change?

The real estate development industry isn't exactly a hotbed of innovation. The business model really hasn't changed in decades. It travels through a tried-and-true process of dirt to owned property to construction and homes. There are no real competitive threats to that model. No one has come along and disrupted it by finding a way to build first and then buy land or maybe just build floating homes that don't need land. There certainly are a lot of new ideas about how to build and what to build, but those come from the design and architecture community; they're the thinkers, not the developers of land. The industry is also heavily dependent on investors who don't like risk. They don't want "different."

The objective of the Bright Building in Joy Experiment terms quickly started shifting from having an idea for an all-electric condominium to showing it actually could be built in a way that was just as financially rewarding as conventional approaches. To truly demonstrate that, HIP had to not only show profit was possible but had to openly share its approach to technology and infrastructure.

Scott: I'm very proud of what the Bright Building is in terms of a unique structure. I'm equally proud of our open-source behaviour. Not only did we show new ideas were possible, but we also demonstrated that in an industry that tightly follows the status quo playbook you could turn ideas into reality and mitigate risk. The building's 228 units sold out in four weeks during the height of Covid uncertainty. To foster creative confidence, we also took a "no-secrets" approach to all that we've learned. We're happy to share the lessons and innovations we've discovered along the way. I'm thrilled to see that other developers are now planning similar projects. That's not competition — that's ecosystem success.

Welcoming the industry into this project's activities is clearly a big step, but the challenges society faces in terms of carbon emissions requires many more big steps and a few leaps. Not only would the Bright Building have to evolve into a bright industry, but it would also have to show it could change the behaviours of the people who live in the building. After all, we still need to get better at switching off lights and turning down air conditioning, even if our homes are built with environmentally friendly construction techniques. HIP also had to invite the Bright Building residents into the Joy Experiment.

Paul: A number of years earlier I was involved with naming Canada's first net-positive-carbon office building — "evol1," a 97,000-square-metre building in the University of Waterloo's tech park, created by the Cora Group, a Waterloo-based commercial real estate developer. To achieve this success, Cora worked in conjunction with Sustainable Waterloo Region (SWR), a social enterprise non-profit that helps the local business community, and Waterloo Region, become more environmentally and economically sustainable. During my naming engagement, I got to know Tova Davidson, SWR's executive director, and shortly after evol1 had its grand opening Tova gave me a tour and talked about the scope of the undertaking. Two of her statements really stuck with me. First, all the technology in the building was pre-existing. Nothing new had to be invented to build the first net-positive office building. It just had to be assembled in a uniquely creative way. The second thing Tova explained to me was that the real success of the building would depend on the behaviours of the tenants. A green culture would have to be nurtured, structured, and constantly maintained. She followed this statement by explaining the detailed culture-building partnership SWR and the Cora Group were embarking on.

I'd like to award evol1 with a Joy Experiment trophy. We'll have to work on that.

The activity of SWR stayed in my head, and when Scott started talking about an idea that would eventually become the Bright Building, I suggested he pull Tova into his resource circle. The SWR team built a structure that's emblematic of the collaborative ethos we've been talking about in this chapter. Here's how Tova describes it:

> The work that SWR does, as a strategic intermediary, is the foundation of how we bring together the need for community building with the systemic change that sustainability requires. This unique role in the community means that we are able to convene partners, stakeholders, decision-makers, and those impacted, with the business community, other social service agencies, and industry experts, all contributing their unique gifts to the creation of a better future. The end result is a community that is more prosperous, connected, equitable, and sustainable. More importantly, the process itself creates joy, connection, and innovation. This is due to the foundation of collaboration, inclusivity, and a shared desire for a better future.

The SWR partnership is living up to this description and has allowed the Bright Building to start working on its own green culture program.

HIP and the Bright Building joined SWR's network, which includes researchers, entrepreneurs, the University of Waterloo, the Accelerator Centre, and Wilfrid Laurier University, all of whom offer a community approach to building a clean economy. As a result of this further expansion of open-source behaviour, HIP is able to incorporate a new software technology into the Bright Building called InCharge. This phone-based app will allow people to monitor their daily hydro consumption and control their costs. The technology will become part of the building's living behaviour because it's also a security system and platform for condo community communications. Over time, more green culture behaviour activities will be added to the Bright Building and more learnings will be shared with SWR and the community at large. We like the way Tova describes this experience: "It's great having the Bright Building as part of our network because the future of our region, and the world, is through leveraging leading-edge technology and knowledge to create a community willing to embrace invention and change."

This story and chapter illustrate the need for a bolder approach to collaboration. As we mentioned earlier, cities are habitats for humanity and are every bit as interconnected as nature's habitats. So new forms of city building will require equally interconnected collaborations. It just might be that the biggest and most needed invention of all of our times is the shift of collaboration from being a tactic to being the goal.

Together we're just more fun.

CHAPTER TWELVE

The Streets Should Be Free

In the Bob Dylan documentary *No Direction Home*, we get a close-up into one of the unique features of great cities — the creative cluster. The film takes a deep dive into the New York City neighbourhoods of Greenwich Village and SoHo in the 1950s and 1960s. The camera lens chronicles the atmosphere of the clubs, coffee shops, and lofts that hosted an explosion of art, music, and literature that still drive aspects of modern culture to this day.

Those neighbourhoods were the birthplace of Dylan, Andy Warhol, Jack Kerouac, Donald Judd, Allen Ginsberg, Lou Reed, Patti Smith, Truman Capote, and many more. We acknowledge that SoHo and Greenwich Village may not have been the physical birthplaces of these people, but that was where they became the earth-shaking cultural figures we now know. That was where Robert Zimmerman of Hibbing, Minnesota, became Bob Dylan. It was where Andrew Warhola of Pittsburgh became Andy Warhol. These people became cultural icons and created great things for three dominant reasons:

- They were very talented and worked really, really hard at their crafts.
- They were constantly around one another, collaborating, competing, copying, and feeding off each other's ideas and talents. Bob Dylan could sit in a club and listen to jazz played by Thelonious Monk and be surprisingly influenced.
- They were fortunate enough to have all lived together in a cheap area of the city that afforded them the luxury to experiment, fail,

Ideas, invention, and local ingenuity don't thrive in trendy spaces; they thrive in spaces that are affordable enough to allow failure.

and experiment some more. No one needed to be an overnight success financially.

For a long time, SoHo was really a place of empty factories and warehouses. Some didn't even have hydro, but artists, musicians, writers, and inventors were looking for cheap places, so they moved in. Whenever a group of people start focusing on an objective beyond the vision and desires of current social and economic trends, they seek out how to get away from the controls of the status quo such as the need for money to pay rent. They might speak in rebellious terms, such as "I get to do what I want" or "I don't have to please anyone but me," but an underlying thought in those statements is the freedom to fail a few times because you don't have to pay $4,000 per month for a condo with marble countertops.

Paul: When I watched *No Direction Home*, it became very clear to me how important these neighbourhoods and the connection between diverse groups of people was to the growth of innovative thinking. All those minds were connecting on Bleecker Street and meeting in dirt-cheap artist lofts and gritty places such as the Gaslight Cafe, the Village Vanguard, and the Fanelli Cafe. You could still hear the energy of that era in the voices of people being interviewed for the film. With brightness in their eyes, they described how they explored ideas without the crushing concern of commercial output. They had time and space that helped to create a "blurry" environment where ideas could grow. It was a good kind of blurry.

There are still a few glorious holdouts of that era in Manhattan such as the Argosy Book Store. Now housed in a six-storey building surrounded by skyscrapers and super skyscrapers, Argosy is the oldest independent bookstore in New York City and still focuses on selling a marvellously eclectic selection of books to book lovers. Before Patti Smith was turning punk rock into poetry, she worked in this bookshop. The third generation of the family is running the business, one can assume, for the love of ideas within the books. It certainly isn't for the money, because the path to profit would be in ripping it all down and putting up a super-duper skyscraper. We love that the Argosy is still around, but even though it can claim Jacqueline Kennedy, former presidents, and innovative greats such as Stephen Sondheim as customers, one holdout doesn't a creative cluster make.

I began thinking about where those creative clusters are today, not just artistic but any category of thought and innovation. I don't mean

Falls Park on the Reedy

GREENVILLE, SOUTH CAROLINA, WITH A POPULATION OF A little over 70,000, is the sixth-largest city in that state. It's home to three universities, the North American headquarters of Michelin, and the Clemson University International Center for Automotive Research. As a result, Greenville was also the fourth-fastest-growing city in the United States between 2015 and 2016, according to the U.S. Census Bureau. You could say it's the mid-sized city poster child.

To get to that kind of national profile, Greenville had to make a few bold moves to become a place that could feed people's need for joy and businesses' desire for engaged and vital workers. One of those bold moves was to bring its downtown back to life by building a 13-hectare park that went on to win national attention.

Greenville, like many North American cities in the 1970s, saw its economy falter and its downtown core hollow out due to the exodus of many retailers. Local leadership developed many projects to turn things around, including a convention centre and a new downtown library, but it was the creation of Falls Park on the Reedy that gave the city an iconic symbol (the Liberty Bridge), a beautiful urban community gathering spot, and a distinctively vibrant and livable urban centre.

Gems like Falls Park don't just appear overnight, and rarely is land in the downtown core of cities just waiting to be easily converted into sources of joy. Falls Park took vision, the kind that can see what could be there rather than settling for what existed.

Hidden beneath a highway bridge erected in 1960 was the physical birthplace of Greenville by a waterfall on the Reedy River. Some forward thinkers began to imagine this unlikely and difficult-to-convert site as a truly unique natural asset to a city trying to move beyond the problems it was facing. Of course, creating an award-winning urban park on this site would require the removal of the bridge and that idea, not surprisingly, was blocked by some city leaders who felt this was a silly idea and a waste of taxpayers' money.

This group made dire predictions of traffic disasters for a park they felt no one would ever use. But the miraculous happened. The bridge came down, the traffic chaos didn't happen, and the park was built, containing a 108-metre-long pedestrian suspension bridge that curves around the waterfall and gives the public an unobstructed view of this natural and culturally historic site. The park also contains a collection of public gardens, and each summer it's home to the Upstate Shakespeare Festival. The $13 million investment to build Falls Park on the Reedy returned $150 million in private investment directly adjacent to the park in just 18 months. The condos, hotels, and restaurants draw tourists and, more importantly, young people to the city, who stay because of the vibrant atmosphere. We think taxpayers got a handsome return on their investment.

Sometimes joy doesn't come easy. It has to be fought for, and occasionally a dusty old highway bridge needs to be removed. §

institutional clusters set up to focus on efficiency and maximize profitable outputs. I mean raw, unknown world-class talent pushing boundaries in defiance of the odds. What's the SoHo of today? Silicon Valley comes to mind when it was a place where kids built computers in their garages, but who can afford a garage anywhere near San Francisco today? I'm not an expert on the subject, but I really couldn't come up with a place where the next big undefinable thing is "happening." That thought bothers me because this world needs that kind of defiant and inventive explosion more than ever.

About 20 years ago, Richard Florida had a different take on how invention ecosystems could be supported. He used a new term, *the creative class*, and imagined how these people would be attracted to neighbourhoods with cool coffee shops, art galleries, and museums. His approach was strongly data-driven and felt formulaic as he predicted what combination of demographics would become the creative class and what these creative people wanted in their environments. It seemed to us that creativity carries a lot of wonderful attributes, but predictive formulas are likely not one of them. Florida's approach could be interpreted as an attempt to speed up the creative-cluster process. In hindsight, he might have been replacing the seemingly slow and inefficient cheap space and "freedom-to-fail" model in favour of cool space and faster economic benefits.

Florida's predictions ended up being a mix of right and wrong. A version of the creative class — people primarily white, educated, well off, and working in the tech industry — clustered in stylish, trendy areas did ignite creative economies. But the benefits didn't extend much past their own groups. Their success drove up housing prices, and many cities simply became too expensive for others, including the innovators and Dylans of our time, to live in.

While inventors may get pushed out of overheated real estate markets, they don't disappear, and their "freedom-to-fail" model never stops supporting them. Hand in hand, they go searching for cheap, or better yet free, rent. As an example, as Manhattan faded in terms of creative glory, Brooklyn became the new blurry area of invention, and when it became too expensive, innovators moved on, and Detroit became the new frontier of possibility. The ideas that propel us beyond the status quo often come from areas beyond its reach — on streets that are almost free. And that could be very good news for smart mid-sized cities.

Scott: Today, SoHo is home to only the richest of the rich. For the most part, it feels as if only millionaires can live in Manhattan. Superstar cities are losing their ability to offer the world what it really needs — new ideas. What the Richard Florida experience taught me was that efficiency at the price of freedom to take risks is bad for creativity. And to a certain extent, it's bad for city building, as well. Inventiveness comes from diversity, and that's what cities naturally offer ... or offered in the past.

I see the time we're in as a wonderful opportunity for mid-sized communities like Waterloo Region, if we choose to grab the moment. Communities our size haven't reached the point of cost-of-living overload that superstar cities have experienced. But to succeed, we need urban design guidelines in step with diversity rather than rigid conformity. No city can become a true creative cluster or offer solutions to the divisive social issues of society if its approach to urban design is always efficiency and sameness. We need space for the infrastructure of some joyfully messy creativity.

The most critical piece of that infrastructure is the space and financial freedom to experiment and fail. Failure teaches you everything you need to know about succeeding. Steve Jobs and Albert Einstein failed far more often than they succeeded. SoHo, with its low-rent lofts with high ceilings and big windows, offered more than just sunlight. It gave raw talent the freedom not to be financially successful right away or perhaps not focus on financial accomplishment at all. The result: the words, songs, and paintings that 70 years later still lift our spirits or make us cry beautiful tears.

To be blunt, if Steve Jobs didn't have his parents' garage free, we wouldn't have iPhones.

If we acknowledge that the most important output of the innovation economy is new ideas, and that cities are the engine of creating them, then we must invest in our cities differently. The cool coffee shops, bars, bike paths, and museums Richard Florida recommended may or may not be mandatory, but I firmly believe we need to create space for creativity and invention that acknowledges the historically proven need for cheap real estate and without needing the output fully defined. We just have to acknowledge that invention and new ideas are a messy business and commit to them.

Free Streets is a Joy Experiment focused on crafting space for creativity and invention through a bold effort to change zoning laws so that creative clusters needn't scatter in the wind the moment communities start to prosper. And of all of HIP's experiments, we hope it's the one that helps lead a fundamental shift in how communities view the allocation of space and its relationship to creativity — the industry of our future.

Here's a look at the current reality of city planning and building. Many people hope the growth of real estate development in our urban cores, including large condominium towers, will help our cities become more competitive and appealing at a social level. However, current zoning and planning policies for condominiums across the country usually require the street level to be dedicated to retail usage. These policies were developed and entrenched decades ago when there was a belief that retail was the primary tool for activating streets. So today, developers of condos must shift mandatory amenity spaces away from the ground level to the upper floors, producing "backyards in the sky." Developers follow a required formula that demands a certain square footage of amenity space be built based on the square footage of living space in the building. This can often result in amenity spaces being the size of small YMCAs, but they're in private hands and inadvertently encourage residents to remain in their buildings rather than exploring their larger neighbourhoods. What gets created isn't public amenity space for growing downtown city cores. It's

A moment full of potential.

> **We just have to acknowledge that invention and new ideas are a messy business and commit to them.**

private "clubs" exclusive to a few and used by virtually no one.

Alongside this movement, new tech companies internalize their amenities such as gyms, cafeterias, and lounges in office buildings. Their goal is to encourage staff to stay in the buildings as much as possible. Meanwhile, the retail spaces, mandated for the street level of condos, sit empty because of no pedestrian traffic and the general decline of bricks-and-mortar retail due to e-commerce. If this space does get leased, it often goes to national retail chains with generic offerings because it's too expensive for local businesses.

None of this form of city building, much of which is mandated by city policy, is conducive to creating vibrant communities or creative clusters. It's a massive waste of urban investment and generates empty spaces, isolated living, and sameness. It's not that there aren't potentially cool communal places to hang out or potential spaces for innovative minds to invent, it's just that there are costs and barriers everywhere.

Perhaps this is the inevitable and ultimate state of existence caused by North American immigrants' centuries-long desire for private space. That perceived need among those who came to this continent has been built into our social psyche since the *Mayflower* set sail. People got on ships to get away from Europe's problems, and once they set foot in the New World, where Indigenous people already lived, they began to put distance between themselves and have done so ever since. When the first cities got crowded, Europeans and others crossed rivers. Then they travelled across the prairies and even the mountains, all to get away from everyone and have their own private space. We're masters at dividing land and our lives. That may be a bit of an overstatement, but there's a grain of truth embedded in it.

Free Streets offers a different philosophy and approach. It's an exercise in reshuffling the deck and a demonstration of what can happen when a community changes its perspective on what's deemed important, such as acknowledging that the people who tend to make the pulse of a city exciting — the artists, musicians, and inventors — have small incomes yet play a large role in building identity.

Targeting condominium tower developments, Free Streets rethinks what our zoning laws encourage, or discourage, in terms of a healthy urban core. First and foremost, it does away with the demand for retail on the street level and instead allows real estate developers to offer rent-free space to tenants of their choosing as long as they qualify as creative entrepreneurs — art studios, performance spaces, start-up tech clubs, kitchen studios, et cetera. That would add to a city's cheap

Free Streets is one example of a collaborative approach to vital city building.

space inventory for creative invention, putting all that energy on display to the community. Developers would also be given the freedom to move the remaining amenity space closer to the ground level where it could connect to these other activities. Perhaps a "creative studio" lounge designed for those working in the Free Streets space might link with the tenant lounge.

We think the result would be a big win for everyone. Residents would feel that their ground floor and neighbourhood are their most important amenities, where the lines between private and public space blur with stimulating space for fresh new businesses to experiment and grow in a way that's more visible to the public. Invention, creativity, and stimulation would fill the streets. Pedestrian traffic would increase, which would improve the viability of all retail and hospitality vendors.

This program wouldn't add any additional costs to real estate developers, since they're already required to build and furnish these amenity spaces. Any expenses incurred in street-level planning and activation would be offset by gaining more space on the upper levels of their buildings for apartment units, sometimes as many as 12 or more, which would add to the developer's bottom line and increase the tax base of the city.

Most importantly, Free Streets sets an example for how the public and private sector could collaborate in building the new type of amenities required for the rebirth of mid-sized city urban cores and focusing on the people, businesses, and activity that provide the biggest return on investment from a community identity and energy perspective.

Paul: During a trip to Berlin, Germany, I was able to experience the energy and life a Free Streets type of experience can offer. Like many European cities, a large part of Berlin was made up of apartment buildings containing courtyards that often included smaller buildings. In the Wall years, the centre of Berlin, Mitte, was a bit of a ghost town because much of it was East Berlin.

When the Wall fell, this area and the vacant, mysterious courtyards were quickly inhabited by the city's creative community. It became an affordable area for experimentation, innovation, and creativity. Over the years, that creativity created excitement and interest. It attracted people. Today, the area is somewhat gentrified. Many courtyard buildings contain trendy and innovative restaurants, but somehow the city has still managed to hold on to space for raw creative ideas. The streets, unlike almost every downtown core

I know of, are bucking the declining retail trend. Storefronts are full of vibrant shops that tend to have local content. Yes, there are some national and international brands, but there are many pockets of alleyways full of weird, wonderful, and unique experiences and retail such as designer clothing shops where the making and selling of clothes intermingle.

Mitte suggests that a future of empty streets and vacant storefronts can be avoided.

Free Streets aligns with the PLAY, LIVE, WORK model when you consider that play can be more than playing with Frisbees in a park. Play is also the freedom to follow passions, to do what you feel you're meant to do. In fact, there's no greater joy than being lost in the pursuit of a passion. It's even better when you're collaborating. There's also a lot of joy in living in an environment where you can experience other people's passions. It's a "high octane" way of connecting with the energy of a community and growing with it. All of this can lead to the development of a city that has the somewhat magic ingredients to create the next big thing. Filling empty retail space with joy isn't bad, either.

HIP brought the Free Streets model to city decision-makers, and we're prepared to persuade them by taking the lead and demonstrating success. When the Gaslight District in Cambridge opened, there were 10 studio spaces made available to select artists for free where they could experiment, create, and sell in full view of the public. We not only believe this will help the arts community but also think it creates a wonderful and invigorating public space. As well, the all-electric Bright Building condominium project will bring its heavy community focus to life with a Free Streets makerspace on the ground floor.

Part of what we're trying to demonstrate with these experiments is that real estate developers have a vested interest in ensuring our downtown cores have critical density and can offer stimulating experiences. This is the ecosystem for their future success. Free Streets allows real estate developers to allocate their existing project investments in a way that contributes to that type of public environment.

Ultimately, Free Streets illustrates a new model in which the private and public sectors can strategically collaborate to tackle the challenges that face cities with the rapidly declining bricks-and-mortar retail sector, and to build a competitive advantage for attracting and retaining the best talent in the innovation economy. Right now, Free Streets addresses opportunities associated with condominium towers, but its approach and philosophy, in the hands of other people, in other cities, tackling other challenges, could convert other spaces into neighbourhoods of inventive thought and community identity.

CHAPTER THIRTEEN

Becoming a Congregation

In *The New Localism* by Bruce Katz and Jeremy Nowak, the authors write: "Cities and other localities can craft and deliver better solutions to hard challenges since they match problem solving to the way the world works — integrated, holistic and entrepreneurial rather than compartmentalized and bureaucratic."

Katz and Nowak suggest that cities are a critical structure for building solutions for today's problems. We love the previous quote and the whole book. *The New Localism* is, in our humble opinion, important reading for civic and business leaders who want their communities to achieve their full economic and social potential. One of the strategic tenets of the book is the need for information and economic collaboration between government, private sector, and educational institutions within cities. We think the theme of collaboration runs even deeper than those structures.

The integrated and holistic approach that Katz and Nowak discuss must stem from, or be strongly supported by, united and inclusive groups of citizens. Unifying a community, in an emotional and tactical sense, provides the level of energy and political support needed to drive Katz and Nowak's vision. This is the reason we focused some of our Joy Experiments on identity celebration. Our logic suggests that if the collaborative nature of cities is critical to fulfill their potential and generate positive change in the world, then it has to be held together by a community as aligned and as enthusiastic as a … congregation.

To create the type of cities *The New Localism* outlines, and that we need, city builders from

> **The economic and social success of cities will increasingly rely on integrated, holistic, and entrepreneurial collaborations.**

all backgrounds and institutions will need to move beyond the basic concepts of appeasing taxpayers or attracting employers and workers. They need to think about what they can do to foster shared values and a willingness to collaborate at a citizen level.

It's true there's a growing desire among the general population to feel more connected to their communities. Depending on the path you take through this book, you may have already been introduced to the trend and know there are many new obstacles to achieve that unity. A lot of our social fabric has been ripped in the opposite direction because of the negative effects of social media and the digital world. We aren't preaching that all technology is bad, but it's a well-documented fact that much of it isn't good for our mental health. Technology can connect us, but the industry is rapidly building the infrastructures of isolation.

Consider this startling thought: a generation is being raised in an environment where their primary relationships are developing online within the context of fabricated realities. It's also fair to say this is affecting, to a certain extent, older generations. What we mean by fabricated realities is that the subject matter, values, and priorities that link people online are curated by algorithms designed to, frankly, influence our behaviour and sell us stuff whether that be a product or a point of view. There's a saying about technology and media: "If you don't pay for the product, you are the product." While the origin of that quote is hard to pin down, there isn't much debate about how it describes social media users. These platforms serve up highly engaged and aggregated audiences to advertisers by creating comfortable and tailored realities to captivate social media users. As a result, and at a growing rate, the most meaningful realities we carry with us are fabricated. Instead of our sense of reality grounding us, it becomes yet another puff of smoke that in the wrong hands divides us.

Additionally, our ability to meet all our needs with hardly ever venturing into public (queue the Uber Eats commercial) means we have fewer moments to build flesh-and-blood connections with people, weakening our social skills due to disuse. In a March 2020 *Atlantic* article, "The Coronavirus Could Cause a Social Recession," by Vivek H. Murthy and Alice T. Chen, this trend was referred to as a "social recession" and defined as "a fraying of social bonds that further unravel the longer we go without human interaction."

What we're doing with technology defies the logic and reality of who we are as humans and what makes us that. Simply put, we're social creatures. Throughout the whole history of humanity, people have been in family structures and communal groups. Are we losing the social skills and common perspectives to be the collaborative communal web to support *New Localism* definitions of successful cities? Judging by cancel culture and other trends, it's fair to say those skills are certainly in decline.

The best cities have always been built to facilitate social activity. That's why they're the source of tolerance, creativity, invention, and humanity. And that's what we need right now because the challenges of globalization, climate change, and diversity aren't going away. Yet creating the social foundation for those cities has become increasingly difficult. Our recent Covid-19 experiences have only accelerated these dire social recession effects. The question we must ask ourselves is this: Are we aggressively responding to these challenges by creating the infrastructure that will result in the cities we need, or are we still prioritizing and planning for cities of the past?

Addressing today's realities concerning city spaces, Danish architect and place-making expert Jan Gehl says in the book *New City Life*:

> Now — with the proliferation of the private auto, suburban shopping malls, numerous home entertainment offerings, spacious backyards and many other incentives for us to simply stay at home — people venture out in public because they want to rather than because they have to. That creates a new necessity to make city space pleasurable and inviting. Mediocre public spaces will be places no one bothers to visit. Great ones, however, will continue to draw people and foster a sense of urban vitality and community.

Where does collaboration start? We think the battleground for better cities and a better sense of community and mental health starts on the streets and in public spaces. That's where people still have a chance to meet total strangers and learn to laugh and play together.

Scott: Thoughts about collaboration and congregation were in both our minds, though Paul and I hadn't met yet. I was in the process of planning HIP Developments' largest project to date: the Gaslight District in Cambridge, Ontario; the first Joy Experiment and one of the biggest. It's now completed, and we hope it epitomizes how public space can contribute to the idea of congregation. I wanted to really commit to doing something very special for the people and prosperity of Cambridge. The project involves two condo towers, office space, and an event hall, with the aim to create a public square lined with restaurants, art studios, shops, and outdoor cafés. But there's still a bigger social vision to be devised. My intention is to have Gaslight Square be a place where people can come together on a daily basis and rub shoulders with individuals they've never met before as they smile, laugh, and slowly start to define who we are as a city — a place to PLAY, LIVE, WORK.

The battle to save cities and ourselves starts at the street level in co-creative public spaces that allow us to play with strangers and feel a sense of congregation.

I knew what I wanted to do had never been done before, at least not in our community. I also realized I needed help but that support had to come from someone who understood our local culture while at the same time knowing how to push it forward. It was around this time that I met Paul, who had recently developed a public space strategy for the Creative Enterprise Initiative, a collaborative group of private and public sector leaders looking to improve Waterloo Region's cultural vibrancy. His work, entitled *Creative Intersections*, felt as if it was the exact road map needed to turn Gaslight Square into a world-class public space designed to build culture and community.

An example of the "Creative Intersections" effect we wanted to develop at Gaslight are the musical swings in the Quartier des spectacles area of downtown Montreal. The installation is located between the University of Quebec at Montreal's Faculté des sciences and Place des arts, which includes the city's opera house. The art and design studio Daily tous les jours collaborated with the university's science faculty and composer Radwan Ghazi Moumneh to create a co-operative musical experience that opens up the magic of playing music to a wide audience. In true "Creative Intersections" style, the content within the university comes out to play with the public. The swings are illuminated at night, and each one plays the sound of an instrument — the higher someone's swing, the higher the note. Twenty-one swings stretch along a city block, and together people randomly compose music while (re)discovering the fun of swinging in the middle of downtown. The result: a destination always busy, fun, and engaging.

Embedded in this fun is the university's ability to share knowledge and experience with the community, and as a result, the community's opportunity to celebrate the institution. The musical swings show us how play can make social walls porous, and perhaps more importantly, they're an example of the public co-creating. Perhaps people passively enjoy the experience during their first visits, but this is a place to return to, and each time people come back, it's with the purpose of seeing what they and a group of strangers can create.

To anchor Gaslight Square, we decided to go to the source of play and hired Daily tous les jours to create a cultural play area that would have the same effect as the musical swings. We'd already decided that every public art installation on the property had to celebrate the Grand River in some way. As a region, we

Never alone.

needed to learn how to tell our stories in a more extroverted and joyful way. Throughout the world, there are so many great cultural stories about rivers, so we felt it was a natural place to start. Our strategic narrative for the whole project is called "River Lines":

> The Grand River defined our past. Its natural structure gave us a home and beauty. We tamed it and put the river to work for our mills, foundries, and factories. The river rebelled and flooded the community, causing us to come together, be inventive, and form deeper community bonds.
>
> The lines and shapes of the river's bank hold the stories of Nature's River and the Working River. Our stories.
>
> The metaphorical river, The Dreaming River, releases our imagination and allows us to tell the stories of our future. River lines run through us.

Daily tous les jours worked with this story and designed a 24-by-24-metre play area that will trace the 1974 Grand River flood line through the centre of Gaslight Square. That flood line signifies the historical moment on May 16 of that year when a major spring flood put people and property in danger throughout the Grand River Valley. In the downtown Galt area, it caused over $5 million in damage as it flooded streets to the point where motorized boats were used to travel in the downtown core as our community came together in crisis and strangers helped one another.

We want to create an experience where once again strangers will come together, only this time the purpose will be to playfully co-create joy. We also intend to reverse a behaviour born out of the flood. Walls and berms along the river had been made higher and higher, encouraging the community to turn its back on the river. Without the river as a cultural artifact, the community's identity lost its way over the years that followed. *River Lines*, a giant game board with the flood line cutting through the middle, is activated by people standing on specific tiles, which emit light and sound. As numerous people stand on random tiles that connect to one another, the sounds turn into ever-changing music. The dancing, play, and laughter that will ensue might be a way for everyone to appreciate their river. But perhaps it's better to let Daily tous les jours express its vision and the desired outcome in its own words:

> The work is a visit ritual for the square. While our use of public infrastructure is more often than not associated with routine, we see our role as makers of rituals, moments lived with intent and meaning.
>
> At the base is a collaborative interaction scenario where people achieve more together than alone. This stimulates informal connections and a sense of collectivity. It acts as an ice breaker between people who don't necessarily know one another, where conversation may follow.... It is designed with

multiple levels of engagement where someone can simply walk and play a tune as they pass by, or further explore all the different ways to create music, alone or together.

Using music is a strategic choice because it moves body and mind and goes beyond language, allowing connections between people across barriers of culture, age, or origins. As cities have grown to cater specifically to different crowds, with a spot for skaters and a spot for toddlers and one for the elders, we feel we need to put extra care into making a public space truly public, connecting multiple generations, and achieving ultimate vibrancy. So we work out a complicated scenario to get people to do things together. And this is most efficiently done through joy. Joy creates a safe space to be together no matter who we are and where we're from. Joy builds trust. And trust builds strong democracies. And strong democracies can do anything.

The artwork is a set of interactive tiles and a sound system embedded into the square's pavement. Step on a tile, play a note; step on two adjacent tiles, play the two notes in a loop. As people participate, a melody is composed. The interactive tiles get closer to one another along the centre of the artwork where the flood line is engraved. As people play music, they are naturally brought together around this historical line, together creating an embodied ritual to pay tribute to the flooding event that marked the community. At a specific time of day … the work comes to life on its own to mark the time and pay tribute to community strength and resilience.

River Lines creates a sense of a congregation out of play and a dramatic moment in our past. The next aspect of the "Creative Intersections" strategy was to continue to celebrate the Grand River while at the same time exposing the public to some of the world-class talent housed in the School of Architecture only a few blocks away.

Returning to the architectural sculpture *Meander* discussed earlier in the book, we see that it illustrates how nature finds strength and sustainability using systems rather than silos. Sustainable problem-solving is also built upon seeing the world as interconnected systems. When people view *Meander* in this way, especially children, the sculpture and the Grand River become a metaphor for nature's networks and how to solve difficult issues in complex environments.

Meander and *River Lines* don't just create congregation and a sense of community through their content. Part of the magic comes from thoughtfully considering the relationships between form, space, and human behaviour. There's a tremendous body of research on the topic of how environments make people slow down, observe, and engage. At the top of the

research list is activity that involves watching other people. We often don't want to admit it, but we like seeing people doing things more than studying nature. So creating an atmosphere in which people can comfortably observe things happening with humans naturally gets more people involved.

We also put a lot of thought into the public spaces that *River Lines* and *Meander* inhabit. *River Lines* is placed in the middle of Gaslight Square. It almost gets in the way when walking though the space. There are no borders or fences. The play area is just there. There are also no cars allowed in the square or even in sight of the pedestrian areas. In this environment, people can act differently. Adults and children don't have to be wary as they walk; they can stroll and wander and easily become absorbed in the play area. No formal invitation is needed.

Around the perimeter of the square, housed in old limestone buildings, are restaurants, shops, and bars, all facing the play area so people can hang out on the fringe and observe while doing their own small group social activity. High up on a wall facing into the square is a digital screen displaying an animated aerial view of the play area and presenting the ground-level activity as if an animated abstract piece of art. People are able to participate at their own comfort levels, but everyone feels part of something communal.

Placed in a public hallway in the building that houses an event space called Tapestry Hall, *Meander* gives the public several ways to observe and engage it. On the main level of the hallway, the impressive sculpture hangs high above under the nine-metre-high wooden ceiling. At that level, people can take in the full expanse and beauty of the work and experience that special sense of awe that often only nature can provide. There's also a second-level catwalk that lets the public immerse itself physically and intimately with the sculpture. At that level, people get so close they can sense the sculpture reacting to their movements. The most important communal aspect of this setting is that both levels are visible to each other, giving the impression that the public is in constant motion around and within the sculpture. In other words, the public is literally part of the sculpture.

Meander spans many aspects of public co-creating important to our Joy Experiments. The first is public experience and a sense of place. Through Philip Beesley's work, we all get to appreciate the Grand River in a unique way, adding to Gaslight Square's cultural importance. But *Meander* also offers another opportunity for unity by helping people explore the nature of creativity and discover their own creative abilities.

Many festivals offer the chance to mingle, which is great, but public activities that encourage people to be more than just the audience are increasingly important. We have to counter the silos of social media and the isolation of technology by continually showing people that "playing with strangers" is a good thing. Thus HIP Developments prioritizes sponsorships that offer a sense of co-creation such as the City of Waterloo's Busker Carnival and the Lumen festival because they're especially famous for turning the audience into the act.

We also need public spaces that on a permanent basis engage people in the telling and co-creating of communal stories. These spaces become the locations we naturally go to when we want to celebrate things like Olympic gold medals and New Year's Eve. They also become the places where we naturally gather during moments of national crisis as we struggle to feel connected. The cities we need aren't going to evolve using the tools of the past. The future is rarely conventional.

[***Meander* illustrates how nature finds strengths and sustainability using systems rather than silos.**]

CHAPTER FOURTEEN

The 15-Minute City

How Can We Get There from Here?

We've been talking a great deal about a new kind of city building for a new and challenging world. In many ways, we're just at the start of a journey of change, and like many of them, there are special destinations along the way that act as holy grails. In the city-building journey, those grails might include more public space, affordable housing, or improved public transportation, to name a few. But there's one hope that's a bit more holy than the rest of the grails because it encompasses most of the ideas on a city builder's wish list: the 15-minute city. All the experts talk about it. All the experts want it. But the path to it often seems unsurmountable.

The 15-minute city concept is fairly simple to explain. Basically, it's constructed around the idea that the most ideal urban life experience involves having everything a person may need — food, work, play, shopping, medical facilities, et cetera — all within a 15-minute walk or bike ride from home. In this scenario, the car is for adventures such as going to visit a relative in another city.

In 2020, Anne Hidalgo, the mayor of Paris, France, built her re-election platform around this philosophy and called it the "quarter-hour city." She had a vision of self-sufficient communities throughout Paris, a collection of true neighbourhoods. The mayor wanted an ecological transformation but was also interested in reducing the stress of Parisians with the help of socially and economically mixed districts. As she said, "My project is about proximity, participation, collaboration, and ecology. In Paris, we all feel we have no time. We are always rushing

[Big challenges like the 15-minute city aren't solved with big solutions. They require a lot of experimentation and collaboration.]

to one place or another, always trying to gain time. That is why I am convinced we need to transform the city so Parisians can learn, do sports, have health care, shop, within 15 minutes of their home." Those bold statements partially helped Hidalgo get re-elected, and we look forward to seeing how she can navigate the creation of this holy grail.

The simple 15-minute, or quarter-hour, city isn't a particularly new idea. It was born in the early 1900s and was called the "neighbourhood unit." At that time, many cities were being formed as a collection of neighbourhoods that focused on keeping people and activity connected. Factories and other work opportunities existed close to where people lived. Perhaps the owners of factories lived slightly to the west of the factories, allowing the prevailing westerly winds to push smoke in the direction of the working-class homes to the east. It was all far from being perfect for everyone, but it was a unit of purpose and connection.

Mixed into these neighbourhood units were corner stores, schools, churches, and other necessities. Perhaps a better description of this structure would be to reference back to the discussion in Chapter 1 and call it a "micro-habitat." Cities became a string of these micro-habitats where the connective patterns were repeated over and over. They were structured very similarly to nature's interconnected systems, and life in these areas reflected that reality. Today, we might look back at daily life in many mid-sized cities and say it was natural compared to the constant rush and struggle of life today.

Neighbourhood units and walkable cities got a boost in the 1960s from Jane Jacobs with her battles against urban renewal and highways cutting through the neighbourhoods of New York City and Toronto. In her book *The Death and Life of Great American Cities*, Jacobs writes: "A neighbourhood is not only an association of buildings but also a network of social relationships, an environment where the feelings and the sympathy can flourish." All these years later, that statement is still music to our ears. With that kind of thoughtful momentum, the 15-minute city idea continued to grow in popularity during the New Urbanism movement in the 1980s as city planners and citizens began tackling the issues related to post–Second World War suburban sprawl.

Today, the 15-minute city's rise to relevance is the result of the Covid-19 crisis. During lockdowns, we all became reacquainted with our neighbourhood units in ways inconceivable only a few years ago. For some, it was a temporary

SUBWAY

Experimentation requires everyone, including citizens and taxpayers, to participate in building for the next generation.

yet surprisingly enjoyable experience with people and places nearby. For others, it's likely not temporary. Covid-19 gave us a glimpse into the future when our homes may also be our workplaces, at least for a few days a week. These experiences have caused many people to become less tolerant of long Ping-Pong-like daily commutes or long drives for basic needs. It's natural to think that as we deal with the Covid-19 reorientation of priorities, the 15-minute city might have found its moment.

We can't help but think that all this presents an opportunity for mid-sized cities, especially those that ring the outer edges of large metropolitan areas. Some call these places satellite cities or the less complimentary term *bedroom communities*. As the population of these cities spend more time in their communities doing more than parking cars after long commutes and going to sleep, there will be a demand for more diversity, opportunity, convenience, and adventure close at hand. The cities that can reorient their urban mix will also capture a greater portion of the population that might consider moving away from larger metropolitan areas by offering them some of the experiences they thought they might have to give up as they left their metropolitan downtowns.

The 15-minute city can sound very much like a fairy tale, conjuring up scenes from the Christmas classic *It's a Wonderful Life*. But solutions need to be found for the social, economic, and environmental challenges caused by unchecked urban sprawl. There's nothing wrong with glancing in the rearview mirror. Sometimes solutions can be legitimately found there.

So why is reaching the 15-minute city solution so challenging? On the surface, it can appear as if the problem we're attempting to solve is an issue of scale, and there's something to be said for that. As much as cities have changed over the past 50 years, many of the core ingredients have remained the same. We still have homes and still build suburbs with backyards. We still have places where we work and a few spaces where we shop and congregate. But the scale of cities has certainly changed considerably. Roads have become highways that sever communities and encourage us to live great distances from the places we work. Connected to those highways are shopping malls surrounded by huge parking lots rather than intimate downtown streets. Scale has changed, but the activities and places are very similar to those of the past.

However, if it were just scale, solutions would seem somewhat straightforward. Creating neighbourhood units would involve the development of a checklist of things needed to support the quality of life such as better food access, improved walkability, and more "third places" or public spaces. Just shrink the scale and things will get better! We aren't attempting to diminish the issue of scale. When scale gets out of balance, the rhythm of a city is also out of kilter. The result makes living feel as if we're constantly swimming upstream. And that's an experience that's very far from joy. But there are other issues that are perhaps more challenging.

Paul: Some of the experts at conferences I've attended suggest that city planning has been focused far too long on the segregation of the urban environment into functional areas, and they feel that until that changes, the 15-minute city will never be achieved, since its organic approach to living flies in the face of functional prioritization.

This seemed like a profound thought with a lightning rod of a term — *segregation*. On the surface, scale might be the problem that needs to be solved. But at a deeper level, the problem and obstacle to a 15-minute city solution is our drive to organize cities for the purposes of efficiency rather than the holistic living humans thrive on. It's hard not to view this approach as yet another example of how we build our habitats in the opposite way that nature does. Nature favours strength achieved through diversity, while we seek economic and social efficiency through sameness. As a result, we constantly struggle with the sustainability of our models.

So we didn't just grow in terms of scale; we also decided that offices should be in one part of the city while factories should be in another, and housing should all be clustered around the outer edges where land and backyards were affordable. No doubt these decisions had good reasons behind them. But they ended up creating two-hour cities where an ordered life rather than an organic one was the rule of the day. And cities segregated for functional reasons quietly and slowly support the segregation of people.

The conversations taking place in these conferences left my mind spinning around the idea that nothing could be more efficient than the 15-minute city, yet, ironically, it was our desire for efficiency that prevented us from making headway.

Even the term *15-minute city* references an efficiency metric — time — which suggests it's all about getting somewhere as fast as possible. Sure, they're just words, but words matter and lead to urban planning that puts monotonous bike lanes beside four-lane roads just so people can technically reach more destinations in the official time limit without using their cars. Surely, the goal should be related to heightened social connection between citizens.

I put this idea to the test with the help of Waterloo architect Ashleigh Crofts. We entered a global 15-minute-city design competition in 2021. Our submission argued that when distance is small, efficiently getting from one place to another isn't all that important; a new design approach that makes moving through the city an achievable social adventure. Our design focused on what we call "social scatterings" that offer routes with mini-destinations and opportunities for spontaneity and connection. A short walk to pick up groceries can include an impromptu hopscotch race and passage through an intimate butterfly garden. Our design turned heads, gained converts, and won third place in the global competition. I think that recognition suggests that it's time to stop measuring our new urban communities by minutes and start counting social encounters and smiles.

Scott: As Paul mentions, an unintentional side effect of our priority on efficiency is the segregation of activity and people. I've witnessed how this issue prevents cities from adapting to change. As our community deals with the changing landscape of retail, there are now empty sections of our cities almost exclusively devoted to retail and big-box stores. These urban deserts are here to stay and will continue to grow. I view these spaces as an opportunity for new neighbourhood units that could be designed to offer all the variety and holistic living of the downtown core without having to be downtown. However, more often than not, my attempts to transform these locations are met with a "those areas aren't zoned for mixed use" response. I appreciate that change is hard and working through it often takes time and a lot of discussion. But these transformational opportunities are classic examples of the need for collaboration between the private and public sectors. I believe the desire for 15-minute cities and other positive city-building goals exist in the public sector, but the approach to collaboration is often stuck in rules and processes that have long outlived their value.

Another example of the need for different thinking and collaboration is affordable housing, which plays a big role in 15-minute cities. As a real estate developer, I'm often asked to create affordable-housing solutions as part of the projects we build. The hope, by various levels of government, is that we can somehow fit these very unique challenges and needs into our business models. I personally know of a lot of developers who want to help solve the affordable-housing challenges of our community, but the harsh reality is that we aren't good at it. At least not on our own. I don't like saying it, but the creation of affordable housing doesn't fit with the realities of how our finances work.

We build things for people to invest in, even when they live in the apartments and homes. We're part of a system that weaponizes housing. Land and real estate of all kinds, including our homes, have become a primary financial instrument to increase wealth. At a corporate level, land is used to extract ever-increasing amounts of wealth from our communities. This system also escalates the tax base of municipal governments. However, the counter-effect of this is an across-the-board shortage of affordable housing in almost all of our cities.

Other developers and I don't want all our efforts to go into exclusively building cities for the purpose of investment. We also want houses and apartments to be affordable homes for individuals and families who will benefit from the social stability that offers. Personally, I also wish to see more of the real estate wealth produced in our community stay there. But these hopes, which are intrinsically connected to goals such as the 15-minute city, require everyone to think and act differently ... together.

Paul: The path to 15-minute cities, which includes diversity via affordable housing, feels pretty daunting when terms such as *weaponized housing* and *segregated cities* get thrown into the conversation. It might seem as if we can't get there from here.

The dilemma of the 15-minute city underscores the necessity to look for experiments rather than airtight solutions that might somehow move us forward while at the same time neatly fitting into current processes. Experiments, large or small, can chip away at the issues and show what can work and what can't. Experiments that give everyone the freedom to turn planning and development inside out can open up opportunities for much-needed collaboration.

Participation in and the embracing of these experiments extends to citizens, as well. As taxpayers, all of us are often unwittingly the cause of the gridlock of municipal politics we find so discouraging. Politicians should be thinking about the needs of current citizens and bravely balancing that against the wants of citizens 25 years from now, because the city-building choices we make today are really the stepping stones to the future. However, that balancing act belongs to the voters, as well, and we sometimes block those steps by wanting nothing to change once we reach our desired home-sweet-home dreams. Having achieved our beautiful homes in new suburbs, we protest against any more cornfields being converted into streets and houses. If we finally find those cool condos in the downtown core, we object to any other new buildings that might get in the way of our balcony views. We pounce upon any project that uses tax dollars on seemingly frivolous activity because we don't want our taxes to change, either.

We need to accept that we're all city builders and that we all have accountability for meeting the very different city-building needs of the next 25 years.

All of these objections puts the fear of lost votes into the minds of politicians, and rather than lead the community, they seek the path of least friction. You could say, "Well, we get what we pay for" when it comes to political behaviour, but in reality a more accurate statement would be "The citizens of the future get what we pay for." The next time you effortlessly cross town using the freeway or have a calming walk through your favourite park, remember to thank the generations before that experimented and paid for those amenities. We need to accept that we're all city builders and that we all have an accountability for meeting the very different city-building needs of the next 25 years.

The point we're trying to make, and that we hope readers start to agree with, is that cities, like every other living habitat, evolve. Yes, rules and bylaws are needed, but not because they're indefinitely infallible. Rules help us make progress to the next big decision point, but at that moment the old rules should become information that helps inform new rules. As with the favourite Covid-19 saying when it comes to cities, "we're all in this together," and that includes the generations that haven't been born yet.

HIP Developments doesn't stay in its lane of traditional real estate development very well, and as a result, often finds itself in interesting partnerships. One of those unorthodox relationships is as a member of the Housing Innovation Round Table (HIRT), a collaborative group of real estate developers and Waterloo Region community leaders. The vision and mission of HIRT states that housing is a human right, and that society can no longer ignore the gap we have in our community. HIRT seeks to collectively facilitate the growth of affordable-housing supply through partnerships and tactical innovation in Waterloo Region so that over time everyone can have a place to call home.

Through this lens of partnership and innovation, the members of HIRT reviewed a request for an expression of interest (EOI) by the City of Waterloo for the development of one of its last significant parcels of land. This was a real frontier within the city limits, not just because the land had never been developed before but also because the city council had clearly expressed its desire that it be turned into a "Complete Community" that fosters public interaction and a strong sense of place among residents and workers that supports community diversity and sustainability. Wrapped into this vision was the need for affordable housing and affordable living that involved aspects of a 15-minute city where most of the ingredients of healthy living were within walking distance or a short public transit ride.

HIRT was intent on ensuring that this "frontier within" become a major step forward in solving Waterloo's fair and affordable-housing challenges. We believed that it was unrealistic to ask the private sector to completely shoulder the solution to affordable and fairer housing. The answer to a fairer city is collaborative, which can sometimes mean that ownership of land, in one way or another, should remain in the community as co-operative, social, or even public property.

So we responded to the EOI with a very different and collaborative path to achieving the objectives within this development. We offered a process that also invited the city and its citizens to participate in a Joy Experiment.

First off, HIRT decided to launch a new social investment fund (SIF) as part of the land development process and HIRT's broader vision. The fund will have a strong social mandate to be involved in land development that advances affordable-housing opportunities and will also be engaged in buying and protecting existing affordable housing. This entity will be able to participate in multiple partnerships in the public, private, and social sectors. It will also provide investment opportunities for community members who seek a respectable return on investment (ROI) and the knowledge that they're investing in the health and success of their own community.

> **Old rules are old. Use them to inform the creation of new ones.**

This type of new model provides an opportunity to change the financial landscape to one that better supports affordable-housing initiatives. The complete communities that so many people desire operate best when broad, community-wide, and long-term strategic objectives are in place. The fund is one way to avoid the shorter-term limitations of private capitalism. Most importantly, the SIF model helps keep profits in the community or even reinvested in other community projects. It's a chance for financial collaboration — allowing levels of government and local citizens to invest in the health and fairness of their cities.

Second, we took a very serious and fresh look at what's required to build successful complete communities. These types of habitats work well when attention in the planning and design process is paid to how people interact with what will be built and how it can meet their physical, economic, and social needs. It's worth repeating the Jane Jacobs quote here: "A neighbourhood is not only an association of buildings but also a network of social relationships, an environment where the feelings and the sympathy can flourish."

Our submission offered a fluid design vision and a community engagement process that would ensure that diverse voices of lived experience would continually influence design and construction decisions. We offered to form a community consortium with private sector and social not-for-profit members who could offer a real-world knowledge base of real estate and social needs.

While we delivered a high-level plan for a fair housing community, which included a mix of supportive and affordable rental units and attainable homes, our real offering was a process that focused on "co-creation" with the community rather than just a feedback mechanism. It wasn't just a step toward creating a complete community. The process would actually be the first manifestation of the community we hoped to build.

Unlike other Joy Experiments in which the measure of success was action and the creation of something the community could react to, the HIRT proposal was an effort focused on voicing a new process or path that could change the dialogue everyone was having. Plenty had already been written and spoken about the goals of a healthy, inclusive, organic urban lifestyle.

What was missing was an articulation of an equally inclusive process. Moving beyond the appearance of public participation to making it a mandatory criterion was the only way to get where we all wanted to be in the future from where we stood today.

A co-create and co-invest model can provide the lived-experience knowledge to help decision-makers apply new criteria to their planning processes, as well as new financial partnerships to support a whole new set of city-building actions. The HIRT proposal, while not chosen as the winner for the project, has succeeded in letting the genie out of the bottle. The conversation is no longer "Until things change …" or "We'll never be able to …" We now seriously start to renegotiate how affordable homes are created by saying, "We have choices. We can work differently to achieve a different outcome. We can share knowledge, resources, responsibilities, investment returns, and joyful outcomes."

It's our hope that the next opportunities will be treated differently.

Merrily riding along.

CHAPTER FIFTEEN

Community Is the New Faith

If you feel really stressed out these days, it's probably because society is really stressed out. Every country, city, and industry is dealing with a lot of social, economic, and political upheaval. We've touched on many of the factors at play, but it's worth repeating one more time. We are feeling the anti-social implications of social media and the pains of an economic system that isn't working as well, or as fairly, as we know it must in order to create sustainable prosperity for the majority of people.

In moments like these, we tend to reach out and lean on, as John Lennon's song title puts it, "Whatever Gets You Thru the Night." Often that bit of hope can be in the form of a wall to protect us or a bridge that can help us move to a better place. Interestingly, Lennon called the album that song appears on *Walls and Bridges*. Sometimes the happenstance of the creative mind can see very far into the future. We really are at a point where so many decisions are a choice between walls and bridges.

In the past, what might have gotten us through the night would have been faith in big things such as religion, national identity, or paternalistic leaders. Some people still place trust in those things, but a lot more of us view those cultural structures as part of today's problems, and our faith has waned or even vanished. Large political and social organizations are very slow-moving, and as a result, slide dangerously out of step with the rapid change caused by technology and global economies. It's not hard to see how the Amazons and Facebooks of the world seem to be calling more shots than

We really are at a point where so many decisions are a choice between walls and bridges.

governments. It's also not hard to feel the implications of these changes in our daily lives.

As we move away from these old and rigid institutions, society appears to be looking with fresh eyes at the potential role of our cities and the neighbourhoods where we live. Rather than parking our faith in vast concepts, we're starting to think smaller, seeking hope at a local level. People are putting more faith in the idea of "community," an altruistic place where a person can feel connected to something of value and in control. Another way of putting it is: *community is the new faith.*

We view this early trend optimistically. That desire and the need it fills have the potential to create great change at a grassroots level. But the timing of this newfound interest in community is bad, or at least a little unfortunate. For a very long time, the priorities of Western society have slowly dismantled many "community" structures as part of an effort to find the most efficient way to achieve individual convenience and gratification at the price of collective good. To illustrate this point, let's look at organized religion as a social structure that has traditionally given people a physical and social sense of belonging in their neighborhoods for thousands of years. That role has vanished from many of our lives. Consider the following statistics:

- A 2018 Pew Research Center survey found that 64 percent of adult Canadians felt religion had a less important role in their country and communities than it did in the previous 20 years.
- Canadian census data from 2011 showed that 3 in 10 Canadians say they're either atheist (8 percent), agnostic (5 percent), or "nothing in particular" (16 percent). The data also indicated that the "religiously unaffiliated" category increased from 4 percent in 1971 to 24 percent in 2011. We can assume that number has continued to climb since that date.

Throw into the mix the decline of Boy Scouts, Girl Guides, glee clubs, pool halls, business clubs, corner stores, or even the absence of the mail deliverer who knew everyone. What foundational social structures have replaced these things? Sure, we sign our kids up for every sport under the sun, but that's become more of an exercise in checking off the boxes rather than a way of spending quality time with neighbours.

Other communal structures such as government-funded social services and public parks have also fallen into a slow decline as businesses became more global and less local. The big local business benefactor, whose commitment to the community would have resulted in his or her name on sports complexes or libraries,

is becoming extinct. As a result, a larger portion of local taxes is being shouldered by citizens. But let's face it, we as citizens have tended to demand lower taxes at every turn while we focused more on investing in ever-larger backyards and higher fences, so we don't have to spend time packing up to go to a public park. Digital technology has acted as an accelerant of this focus on individual interests and convenience because it creates a view of the world that blurs anything past our own immediate needs.

In many ways, we've got the society we've asked for. So, how are we doing? The good news is we've done all this without driving ourselves into an economic spiral. The bad news is we're in the grips of a social recession.

We're lonelier than ever before!

In 2014, *Maclean's* magazine reported that over 30 percent of Canadians said they felt disconnected from their communities. More people are living alone than ever before, and many people see friends less frequently than in the past. In 2018, a Cigna study in the United States revealed that loneliness was at "epidemic levels":

- Nearly half of Americans always or sometimes feel alone (46 percent) or left out (47 percent).
- Fifty-four percent said they always or sometimes feel that no one knows them well.
- Generation Z (adults ages 18 to 27) get the title "the loneliest generation" and feel they're in worse health than older generations.

So we as a society are faced with a challenge. We can't just "place our faith" in the idea of community; we're going to have to quickly start putting that faith to work building the community we desire because right now it's in decline. Perhaps John Lennon is smiling somewhere as we learn that what will get us through the night is the act of building bridges rather than seeking shelter behind more walls.

Paul: I live in the downtown core near a grand old park — Victoria. On any given day, the park is full of recent immigrant families having picnics that include two or three generations. It's truly beautiful and reminds me of the family picnics from my childhood. One day, on a warm August night, I walked through the park and the song "Family Affair" by Sly and the Family Stone entered my mind through my headphones. I stopped and watched all the kids running through the streaks of twilight sun as it cut through the trees. I knew that at that moment most of the people in my social circle would have been at home, isolated in their backyards or entertainment rooms. While I felt joy because of what I was looking at, I also experienced sadness for what society has lost over the years. I wanted to bring my friends down to the park and start a barbecue using real charcoal and maybe throw a Frisbee around. I wanted to build a bridge to get us all to something better.

What does building bridges look like? Well, the type of action we're talking about involves a fundamental shift in how we choose to organize, prioritize, and fund the places where we live.

Putting it bluntly, we're lonelier than ever before!

It's hard to imagine the "community is the new faith" ideal transpiring without all of us prioritizing common good at least at an equal level to individual convenience. As an example, let's go back to talking about backyards, tall fences, and private amenities. Instead of prioritizing space that belongs only to ourselves, walled in and private, we need to think about the city as our backyard and the joy of engaging with people … even strangers. Today's cities are planned and built with thousands and thousands of small private parks (backyards), which each of us pay for via our property taxes and furnish via our huge mortgages. Individual convenience, yes. Common good, no. Loneliness, most certainly. A healthier, happier, and more socially and economically vibrant life can be achieved with a stronger focus on common-good priorities in which we start to see the city as an extension of our backyard lifestyle.

This common-good approach also applies to transportation, public art, bike lanes, hospitals, and affordable housing. And it involves the *f* word — funding. Priority and funding go hand in hand, and a community worthy of our faith will require a shift in funding at government, business, and individual citizen levels:

- Every faith has its congregation — a group of people united in a cause and belief. That's why we so strongly support the idea of collaborative city building that involves government, private sector, and citizens.
- Every faith has its identity — the stories of its uniqueness, values, and priorities. As cities become the focus of communal faith, the importance of an identity we can all connect to will increase.
- Every faith has its congregational spaces — physical places where people can gather and feel they belong. Public spaces in cities have always provided this value, and today it's needed more than ever.
- Every faith spurs action — especially the experimental kind where people are willing to try what's never been done before, knowing that even if things don't turn out as planned, there will be enough knowledge gained to encourage the next steps of faith in action.
- Every faith has leaders — people who have a way of encouraging others to set aside a slice of their personal advantage for something that pays dividends for everyone.

We believe people in pursuit of community as the new faith are on the right track. Cities, especially mid-sized ones, are small enough to unite people yet big enough to collectively change the world. When we started our Joy Experiments, our focus was Cambridge, Ontario, one portion of Waterloo Region. But we now see Joy Experiments as being something much bigger. They're part of a movement by many everyday people trying to take advantage of this fluid time in society to rebalance things so we can regain some control of our lives and experience a better quality in it. Throughout the world, there are Joy Experiments happening, though they might not be called that. Some are big, some are small, such as parents building community skating rinks or people happily raising funds for affordable housing in their neighbourhoods.

Consider this book an invitation to join the movement. It's a time for things to change from the bottom up. It's a time for a new kind of city building. We invite you to experiment with joy by not erecting taller fences but building bridges from loneliness to collective good. Cities matter because they're the habitat of our humanity and innovation.

Big love.

A Cup of Happiness

THERE'S A CLOSE RELATIONSHIP BETWEEN HAPPINESS AND JOY. We believe a collection of joyful moments results in a sustaining sense of happiness. Perhaps it's the other way around, but if we overanalyze this, we just might kill whatever joy and happiness we have. So let's not do that and just cheer for the people who created The Canvas in England's East London, a self-professed "Happy Café."

In 2014, London seemed determined to be the second-most unwelcoming city in the world, so what better place to build a welcoming Happy Café? The purpose of The Canvas was to unite people with space and support to solve local problems and make life better for everyone in the community. Beyond being a café and a place to take a break with a cup of coffee, it also offered workshop and theatre space. The Canvas ran self-esteem and confidence workshops and hosted an ever-changing handwritten debate on the café walls, encouraging self-expression as a means to build a sense of community. We love the idea of the walls, and perhaps this is where the name The Canvas comes from. The walls were a "canvas" for the thoughts of customers, whether ideas, pleas, stories, or secrets.

Along with this free space for expression comes responsibility for what you write, which raises an interesting thought — happiness, or joy, isn't the absence of responsibility. In some ways, it might require a heightened level of responsibility because joy isn't sustainable if it's harmful to others.

The importance of these smaller connection points in our community can't be underestimated. There are many studies that show that interaction with secondary connections such as the barista at the coffee house or the cashier at the grocery store also add to our sense of belonging and happiness.

A Happy Café might not change the big issues in the world, but it can transform a neighbourhood. §

IN CLOSING

Joy Is Practical

One of the benefits of writing a book is having the last word, or in our case, the last three words — *joy is practical!*

Throughout these pages, we've highlighted trends, discussed issues, reported on experiments, and shared learnings. Meanwhile, quietly in the background, we've been making the case for thinking about joy in practical terms. We suggest that joy isn't a nice-to-have luxury. It's a table-stakes requirement for the future of cities, and nothing is more practical than fulfilling a clear need.

The issues and challenges society faces are hardly insignificant:

- Affordable and inclusive living in a world of escalating have versus have-not disparity
- The unprecedented need for innovative solutions to ever-increasing problems
- Social recession — the growing negative effects of social media on society and individuals
- Shitty capitalism — need we say more?
- Bring your own city — work-from-home trends
- Community is the new faith — the need for actively engaged and united communities
- Retail bricks-and-mortar crisis — the street-level effects of online shopping
- Localism under attack due to the global economy
- Sustainability as it relates to just about everything

Celebrate your city.

When you stack up all these challenges, incremental change to traditional city-building goals won't measure up to the task at hand. We've dug a hole too deep for that. The practical approach is to set new goals even if that requires some unorthodox experimentation to get us to a better place.

For cities, this is a moment of opportunity or retreat, and as we're witnessing in politics and other topics these days, there's very little room for middle ground. The new frontier is within our communities. So let's focus on that opportunity. As we stated at the beginning of this book, cities that create joy will win. The priority formula of PLAY + LIVE + WORK = JOY will make cities the centres of bright minds, collaboration, and invention. Their citizens will be mentally and physically healthier, more united and productive. Those cities will play a bigger role in building what will come next, and we feel that mid-sized communities can capitalize on this moment in time because it's easier for them to adapt quicker than large cities. But it will require boldness because joy favours the bold.

We're assuming our readers fall into three categories of opinion about joy. The first says, "Yes, you had me at hello." The second nods and says, "Maybe. But we need to focus on the capital *P* practical stuff such as dealing with potholes, balance sheets, and health care. We worry about taking away from those things to pursue joy." And the third category stopped reading around the second chapter and got back to doing household chores. To the first category, we respond by saying, "We love you. Tell us your Joy Experiments and let's create together." To the last category, well, since you aren't even reading anymore, we don't need to waste time trying to convince you one more time.

To our "maybe" friends, we'd like to suggest that believing practical need versus joy is a binary decision is misleading. There are many countries that year in and year out prove that joy and prosperity aren't only achievable, they're actually connected to each other. Every year the United Nations Sustainable Development Solutions Network produces the World Happiness Report. It ranks countries on a formula that measures the connections between happiness and development. It includes line items on gross domestic product (GDP) data, life expectancy, social support, perceived individual freedom to make life decisions, management of natural resources, and other capital *P* priorities. In 2020, every Nordic country made the top 10. They had high scores in GDP per capita, economic security, health, education, and management of natural resources. People in these countries felt connected to one another and had a high level of trust in community and government. Canada ranked 11th, and the United States, the richest country in the world, came in at 18.

The top 10 countries haven't sacrificed the practicalities to achieve happiness. They changed their perspectives and priorities regarding common good and reshuffled the deck. With all that going on, they still managed to have prosperous economies.

While joy and happiness aren't completely the same thing, they're closely related. Happiness is a broad or general perspective on one's life. Joy, which comes from moments that make us feel more alive, connected, and vital, is a tool to achieve happiness. Joyous moments add up to a general sense of happiness. The joy examples and experiments we've been discussing are tools for improving the lives of individuals, society, and the world. Together, they form the platform for all of us to shift our perspectives and think differently about cities and city building.

Acknowledgements

This book is dedicated to the passions and drive of Roger Farwell.

Just as we were going to press with the original edition of *The Joy Experiments*, we received word of the sudden passing of Roger Farwell — architect, and more importantly, a Waterloo Region city builder who rejected the greyness of the status quo in favour of the boldness of vibrant cities. As we mention in this book, Roger was the matchmaker who brought us together and the catalyst who started the journey to our experiments in joyful city building.

Our most recent conversations with Roger were a result of asking him to read *The Joy Experiments* and provide a short review of the book. As usual, Roger gave it a great deal of thought. He wanted every word to count. Here is what he had to say:

> There is a popular phrase "The whole world pivots" which can be interpreted as — when one big change happens it can cascade throughout the rest of life. That is certainly true of our times. On the streets, life and living have changed … forever. Disruption now rules the game.
>
> This disruption is profoundly affecting the structure and very purpose of mid-sized cities as societal norms are being reset and the role of mid-sized cities is reimagined as the spawning ground for innovation, creativity, prosperity, and a wonderful place to Play, Work, and Live.
>
> *The Joy Experiments* gives us insight into what might be possible at this pivotal moment in city building by laying out a compelling case that human joy should be seen as a practical objective for cities. The book takes a hard look at the current challenges to "community" yet paints an optimistic path forward.
>
> *The Joy Experiments* invites us all to find the courage to shake off our planning conventions, parochial shackles and reconsider what cities give us and what we give cities.

We're grateful we were able to thank Roger for his support and inspiration while he was alive, but as we get older, we've learned you can never say thank you enough. *The Joy Experiments* is built upon Roger's tenets of city building. And so, this book is our thank you to him for caring so much about our community.

Appendix

The Joy Shift: A New Model for Thinking About, Designing, and Building Cities Differently

Creating joyful cities involves more than adding a new goal to status quo processes. It requires us to ask new questions, turn things upside down, reshuffle the deck, and throw a few friendly wrenches into the works. The Joy Shift Model offers a new sequence of thinking and problem-solving that allows us to take the designing of our cities beyond architectural structures and into public spaces, cultural identity, and social issues.

This model creates the opportunity to respond to the critical issues of our times and replace the current city-building models that prioritize efficiency and the segregation of activities with solutions that better align with human nature behaviour and the supporting of social resiliency.

1. **An expanded situation analysis to include a new set of circumstances:**

- Divided society
- Distrust of institutions
- Social isolation due to technology
- Engaging with, and retention of, youth within our cities
- A growing need for a collaborative society capable of flexible problem-solving
- The need for urban density due to the competing demands of a housing crisis and climate change
- Bricks-and-mortar retail decline
- Talent attraction in the innovation economy
- Growing diversity
- Widening gap between haves and have-nots

2. **View cities as the habitat of the human spirit — the source of creativity, resilience, and inclusion. Successful and healthy cities focus on connecting citizens to one another:**

- When we consider all the infrastructure, processes, and products designed to divide society, we must counter that with a perspective that cities are the moderators of the relationships between citizens.

3. **Ask the question "How does our city play?":**

- Reprioritize the city building approach from LIVE, WORK, PLAY to PLAY + LIVE + WORK = JOY.
- **PLAY:** When you play, you feel joy. You're connected to your surroundings and people. Your body and mind work the way they're meant to work.
- **LIVE:** When people are around places with infrastructure for play, they're engaged, growing, and truly living. They have energy and do amazing things. They take pride in what they create and where they live

- **WORK:** Where talent goes, businesses and investment flows. The talent the economy depends on gravitates to vibrant environments

This new formula calls for a fundamental shift in how we choose to organize, prioritize, and fund the places where we live. It requires cities to invest in a new type of infrastructure that nurtures our human spirit — as much as they invest in conventional civil infrastructure.

Infrastructure for the human spirit turns densely populated urban spaces into joyful and creatively collaborative environments in which tolerance and invention rule the day. It can include:

- Inclusive community identity building
- Redefining the purpose of public space to become engaging places of cultural celebration
- Engaging public art that expresses and encourages community storytelling
- Breaking down social silos by providing *free* spaces for the act of joyfully playing with strangers
- Well-choreographed urban density with a focus on the diversity of the space and its inhabitants
- Public mobility that's viewed as a source of social engagement

4. **Altering the status quo through a willingness to experiment and develop new partnerships between private, public, institutional, and social sectors of society.**

This sequence of thinking and actions can be applied to many city-building tasks from park design to 15-minute city planning, and even to economic development strategies. The new results bring us ever closer to the goal of united and resilient communities.

Join us at thejoyexperiments.com for more ideas, connections, and joy.

JOY

IS PRACTICAL

About the Authors and Illustrator

Scott Higgins

A passionate business and community builder, Scott Higgins is president of HIP Developments Inc. and plays a leadership role in the evolution of Waterloo Region.

Born and raised in Cambridge, Ontario, Scott has roots that continue to grow deep in that community. His desire to achieve both business and community success is the driving vision behind HIP's "Building More Than Real Estate" philosophy. The company actively supports social programs and public spaces that inspire community confidence and define Waterloo Region's future identity.

Scott has more than 15 years of real estate and corporate finance experience, leading both the Toronto-Dominion Bank's and Bank of Montreal's real estate finance activities in Southern Ontario.

Paul Kalbfleisch

Paul Kalbfleisch is a skilled writer, visual artist, and creative business leader. But primarily he is a creative collaborator, placing himself in the middle of projects requiring a strong focus on vision and imaginative design. He has spent more than 20 years in senior roles developing innovative experiential programs and community cultural project strategies. Paul has collaborated with Scott Higgins and HIP Developments for seven years.

Sarah Farquhar

Sarah Farquhar was born and raised in Waterloo, Ontario. She is a Toronto-based illustrator and graduate of OCAD University's Illustration and Design Program. As an emerging illustrator, she is keen to explore new media and all angles of illustration and design. Sarah's work can be found at The Beguiling in Toronto; Shop Maed in Hamilton, Ontario; and on her website sarahfarquhar.com.